evidence, and the rich experience of the authors. While thought provoking and challenging, it is at the same time intensely practical and therefore immediately useful. If you're looking for new ways to share your vision and mission and inspire others to join with you, this book will become your "Bible."—*Geoffrey W. Peters, president and CEO, CDR Fundraising Group, Bowie, Maryland*

"*The Influential Fundraiser* is dazzling! This is the most original piece of work I've seen in the field of fundraising in years—yet it's down-to-earth, wonderfully readable, and eminently practical. If you're involved in fundraising, whether major gifts, legacies, direct mail, telefundraising, or just about any other speciality, do yourself a favor: buy this book! If you follow Bernard Ross and Clare Segal's advice, you'll be sure to raise more money."—*Mal Warwick, author, and president, Mal Warwick and Associates*

"How curious are you? Curious enough to dive into the most recent work of Ross and Segal as they apply their vast insights and intuition into developing professional fundraisers? Packed with common sense, intellectual rigor, and practical steps, *The Influential Fundraiser* explores the psychology of twenty-first century philanthropy and provides key tools for the fundraiser to succeed in this challenging charitable environment."—*Sue-Anne Wallace, CEO, Fundraising Institute Australia*

"Ross and Segal bring fresh perspectives and a host of new ideas to the fundraiser-donor relationship, and *The Influential Fundraiser* itself is an easy and fascinating read that will be useful on many levels. They have pioneered a new approach in fundraising that will be used for decades to come."—*Paulette V. Maehara, CFRE; CAE; president and CEO, Association of Fundraising Professionals*

"Giving will always be intensely personal, so it only makes sense that psychology can play a key role in understanding and approaching donors. *The Influential Fundraiser* is an outstanding volume that can help not just fundraisers, but board members and others, win over major donors and connect them to giving opportunities that will make a difference to the organization and the donor. Fundraisers at every level will find Bernard Ross's and Clare Segal's ideas on how to improve the ways they talk to and win over high value donors exciting and stimulating."—*Lindsay Boswell, CEO, Institute of Fundraising UK*

Praise for *The Influential Fundraiser*

"In this book two of the UK's most influential fundraising thinkers get inside the mind of the donor, and produce some unique, fascinating, and useful insights. Essential reading for the donor-centric fundraiser."—*Giles Pegram, director of fundraising NSPCC UK*

"Breaking news...! You have the potential to be your organization's biggest single competitive advantage...! You can make a real difference in your fundraising by applying Ross and Segal fundraising influential principles. In my job as international vice president for fundraising at one of the largest development organizations working with people with disability in the poorest countries of the world, I need breakthrough and challenging ideas to stimulate and lead our fundraising teams. I definitively found plenty of those in this must-read exceptional book."—*Pierre-Bernard Le Bas, vice president, international fundraising, CBM (Christian Blind Mission)*

"Bernard Ross never ceases to amaze me with his ability to engage people's attention and make individuals and groups want to do his bidding. I have wanted to bottle those secrets for myself. This book shares some of Bernard's secrets, and gives the reader an insight into how to influence people. In today's competitive fundraising environment, this book has to represent a wonderful return on investment!"—*Caroline Harper, CEO, Sightsavers International*

"This book will help you to get right inside the minds of donors—from the way they take in information to how they make vital decisions. It shows you how to overcome objections and, most importantly, how to develop a win-win relationship that will stand the test of time."—*Isabella Navarro Grueter, CFRE, development director, Universidad de Monterrey, Mexico*

"This book is critically important for CEOs, board members, volunteers and fundraisers, and anyone else who seeks to persuade others to support their cause because it truly helps you to get right inside the mind of a donor, board member, or someone whom you seek to influence. It helps you understand how they listen and perceive information and then helps you understand how best to communicate persuasively. It is based on serious research, anecdotal

The Influential

FUNDRAISER

USING THE PSYCHOLOGY OF PERSUASION
TO ACHIEVE OUTSTANDING RESULTS

Bernard Ross & Clare Segal

JOSSEY-BASS
A Wiley Imprint
www.josseybass.com

Published by Jossey-Bass.
A Wiley Imprint
989 Market Street, San Francisco, CA 94103-1741—www.josseybass.com

Jossey-Bass books and products are available through most bookstores. To contact Jossey-Bass directly call our Customer Care Department within the U.S. at 800-956-7739, outside the U.S. at 317-572-3986, or fax 317-572-4002.

Jossey-Bass also publishes its books in a variety of electronic formats. Some content that appears in print may not be available in electronic books.

Library of Congress Cataloging-in-Publication Data

Ross, Bernard, date The influential fundraiser : using the psychology of persuasion
  to achieve outstanding results
    Bernard Ross and Clare Segal. —1st ed.
        p. cm.
    Includes bibliographical references and index.
    ISBN 978-0-7879-9404-4 (cloth)
  1.   Fund raising.   I. Segal, Clare, date- II. Title.
    HG177.R667 2009
    658.15'224—dc22

                                                                            2008039263

Printed in the United States of America
FIRST EDITION
HB *Printing*   10 9 8 7 6 5 4 3 2 1

CONTENTS

ACKNOWLEDGMENTS

Thanks to our outstanding editor, Allison Brunner, whose encouragement and—occasional—cajoling helped make this project a reality. We can teach her nothing about influence she doesn't know. . . .

Thanks also to our many friends and colleagues in The Management Centre who provided help, advice, and challenge when it was needed. Special thanks to Angela Cluff for her support and inspiration.

Finally, thanks to copyeditors Mickey Butts and David Horne for their invaluable advice.

In memory of our dear and inspirational friend
Beto Viesca

PREFACE

Like so many books, this one started in a cafe. The cafe in question was Bertorelli's in London's Soho, and the time almost ten years ago. We were sitting opposite an anxious Caroline, the development director of a leading medical research unit in the United Kingdom. Through our consulting company, The Management Centre (=mc), we had been successfully advising her for some months on how to approach major donors in the United Kingdom and the United States to raise funds for her research campaign.

But on this particular day Caroline had suddenly asked to see us for what she'd called "emergency influence coaching." She had unexpectedly been invited to travel to Riyadh, the capital of Saudi Arabia, in two days' time. There she was to make a ten-minute, one-time, $25 million fundraising presentation to members of the extremely wealthy Saudi royal family and their Western advisers. This was a transformational opportunity for Caroline and for her cause. And she wanted us to advise her on ... well, it seemed like everything:

- What information she needed before she left to make sure she was prepared
- How to frame the case to make it powerful and memorable in ten minutes
- Whether to mention the royal family's previous history of heart disease

- At what point to ask for the donation—the beginning or end of the presentation
- Whom specifically to ask—the advisers or the prince himself
- What she could wear that wouldn't offend
- Where to find out about Muslim philanthropic culture

The list went on.

We had to hold our hands up and say we didn't know the answer to many of her questions because this was a culture and a situation we weren't familiar with. We weren't even sure what really *were* key questions and what were irrelevant. But we gave her our best advice, and we drafted the PowerPoint slides on a slightly stained napkin we still treasure.

Caroline made the presentation. And the good news is she got the money. As important, she came back and gave us challenging feedback on our advice. In some areas we were spot on. In others—particularly, it's sad to say, some of the "surefire" principles we had passed on as established influence and fundraising practice—we couldn't have been more wrong. Here are two simple examples:

- For her presentation, Caroline was required to wear a burka—the head-to-toe robe worn by some Muslim women. All the hints and tips we'd given her on positive body language were wasted, as the only visible part of Caroline was her eyes. Luckily we had also given her advice about eye contact. However, Caroline's feedback made us realize just how much we had underestimated the significance of this subtle communication element. Of course, we knew that different people and different cultures used eye contact differently. But from Caroline's experience we learned there are distinctive *patterns* to this variation. And from our subsequent study we discovered that by matching the *pattern* you can create powerful rapport—even from behind a burka.

- Caroline decided to use the classic "selling the vision" approach for her fundraising ask, or solicitation. But at least half the individuals in the audience looked puzzled. It seemed from her report back that the conventional teaching on solicitation techniques and case structure didn't necessarily work in cultures outside the United States. (Nor, indeed, does it work these days even *within* the United States with the newer, younger venture philanthropists.) So we began to think about how contemporary research from psychology and neurology could help fundraisers construct flexible, *individually tailored* cases. Cases that would have an impact on a wide range of different donors.

That whole experience and several others made us think more systematically about the key ideas behind influence for fundraisers. It made us wonder if there were some principles and approaches that would work in settings ranging from a multi-million-dollar presentation to a royal family for an international initiative, to talking to a local shop owner about giving $200 to the annual carnival pageant, or to persuading the board of a corporation to make significant social investment.

It made us wonder at the same time how donors and their motivations were changing, and if some approaches that worked just five years ago didn't work any more.

This book is the result of that wondering—an organized wondering that turned into a wide-ranging study of influence—what it is, and how it works. It took us several years of action research to develop a robust contemporary model for influence that was relevant for fundraisers keen to get the result their cause needed. Of course our model also had to embody *ethical* behavior toward donors.

We've spent another three years testing our model in every part of the United States and Europe—and then more widely in Ethiopia, Brazil, Mexico, Australia, Thailand, India, China, and many other countries. The techniques have also been tested in

a range of philanthropic fields—arts and culture, education, environmental causes, health care, and international relief.

The insights on how to achieve influence contained in this book are based *primarily* on that distillation of our practical experience as management consultants, coaches, and fundraisers working in the nonprofit world.

But we're happy to acknowledge that we've also built on the work of others. For those of you familiar with psychology, social psychology, and personal development, you'll recognize that we've drawn knowledge and learning from the following:

- Different *psychology* disciplines, from Cognitive Behavior Therapy to Myers-Briggs. These disciplines offer profound insights into the way people make choices.
- From the *personal development* agenda, we've been inspired by Anthony Robbins's work on outcome setting, plus Richard Bandler and John Grinder on anchoring.
- From *social anthropology*, we've drawn on the body language work of Albert Mehrabian and Alan Pease, both of whom have informed our thinking on rapport building.
- From *therapy*, we've been hugely influenced by the late Milton Erickson, especially his skills and insights on empathetic matching and pacing.
- From the *academic research* field, we've drawn especially on Robert Cialdini's work on how to make a lasting positive impact on others.
- From the field of *hypnotism*, we draw on the endeavors of Derren Brown and Paul McKenna, who make their work look like magic.

The techniques we're sharing here are based on practical, real-world approaches that have been tested in tough fundraising situations. Our only claim to fame is that in every case since the cafe example we've *learned* from what worked *and* from what

didn't. Used well, the techniques can help you share complex ideas simply, connect quickly to nervous donors, and build deeper relationships with supporters.

Having said all that we're still keen to keep learning. We'd love to hear what works for you and how our approach might be improved. If you have ideas or feedback, or want to contact us to inquire about training or coaching, log on to www.theinfluentialfundraiser.com or www.managementcentre.co.uk.

Enjoy the book. And more, enjoy the success it will bring to your important work.

September 2008   Bernard Ross and Clare Segal
London

INTRODUCTION

Influence—it's what *donors* want.

The world of fundraising is changing. More and more donors are being turned off by cliched direct-mail packages, their in-boxes are filled to bursting with bland e-newsletters, and they can't bear to listen to another dull speech over a bad meal at a crowded fundraising gala.

Instead, donors want authentic, one-to-one, personal contact that inspires and motivates them to support a cause. They want fundraising messages targeted to them that match the way they think and feel. They want emotionally intelligent fundraisers who understand the way they make decisions.

This book explains how you can give donors what *they* want. It details lessons gleaned from our twenty-five years of practical fundraising experience plus leading-edge research in psychology and neurology. Together these elements provide you with the skills to inspire and motivate—to influence.

So this book is for you if you're a development director, a fundraiser, or a volunteer raising money and looking for approaches beyond the established dogma or tired factory-fundraising formulas. It's also for you if you have to win over donors, colleagues, board members, or uncertain supporters to your mission. Above all, it's for you if you are being asked to achieve challenging results and so need access to higher-level skills to communicate and share your important cause.

A Systematic Approach to Influence

As we said earlier, we've tested all the ideas in the book through our work coaching fundraisers worldwide. This work, plus our wider research, has enabled us to develop a *systematic approach* to influence that's suitable for fundraisers.

Although the model is systematic, it's not simplistic or mechanistic. Instead, it's built around a flexible and powerful approach that takes you through five stages in influence. These involve what we call the *5Ps*—Passion, Proposal, Preparation, Persuasion, and Persistence.

You'll notice that we represent the model as a set of cogs. The cogs metaphor illustrates the following points:

- The elements are all interrelated and interdependent on each other. None is effective by itself—*influence* is a process.
- A small movement in one cog can result in a significant movement or impact elsewhere—influence involves *flexibility*.

In the next sections we take you through this interlocking model, outlining the purpose of each stage and the skills and abilities you'll need to develop. We also offer guidance on where in the book you can find the answers to specific challenges—for example, how to decide exactly what you want from a situation, how to build rapport with "difficult" people, how to handle "no," and how to create an impact with a group of five thousand. You can use this section as a reference source if you're not sure where to look for an insight into a particular issue.

Exploring the 5Ps of Influence

Our work on influence suggests there are distinct stages to go through on the way to successful influence. We've clustered these under the 5Ps:

1. Passion
2. Proposal
3. Preparation
4. Persuasion
5. Persistence

Passion

Success in influence begins with your *Passion* for the cause. One element of this is *emotional engagement*. If the cause doesn't excite and enthuse *you* why should it work for anyone else? But you also need *emotional intelligence* to focus and organize your engagement.

Your own passion is, however, only half the battle. You need to enlist *donor passion* too. This involves understanding donors' *motivations* and addressing their *concerns*—technically called "hygiene factors."

To discover the two key elements that make up *passion* and to begin the process of bringing your donors on board with your

cause, see Chapter Two, "Focusing Your Passion," and Chapter Three, "Understanding Donor Motivations."

Proposal

A *Proposal* is a way of defining both the problem you'd like the donor to help with and your preferred solution.

Your *proposal* should be one that people can *engage* with and respond to. The start in fundraising is often a written document—a case statement or case for support.

- To discover the four choices for framing a case—and which is the most powerful—see Chapter Four, "Making Your Case."
- To learn more about specific types of language that key into donor preferences, see Chapter Eight, "Speaking the Language of Influence."
- To find examples of powerful metaphors to use in written and spoken communications, see Appendix B.

Preparation

Influence is a messy process. Even so, that's no excuse for woolly thinking. *Preparation* allows you to plan ahead for different eventualities and possibilities. That way you minimize the need to think on your feet in possibly mission-critical situations.

Preparation involves lots of hard work. To prepare well you need to do the following:

- Establish a well-formed outcome. If you want to clarify *exactly* what you want to achieve in an influence setting, try using the six-step technique in Chapter Five, "Shaping Outcomes."
- Decide what might be an acceptable range of possible outcomes by working out your LIM-it (*L*ike to get, *I*ntend to get, *M*ust get). Again, to find out more, look at Chapter Five for guidance.
- Eliminate potential negative thoughts or concerns that might get in the way of successful fundraising influence. Find out how to create positive anchors in Chapter Six, "Building Self-Confidence."

Persuasion

Persuasion is about understanding the psychological preferences and filters that will encourage your donors to say "Yes" (or reinforce their possible "No"). The key is to respond flexibly and creatively to donors' needs and interests. The three chapters that might help here are concerned with the following:

- *Rapport:* We are often very different from the people we are trying to influence. By understanding the main communication channels and especially the importance of body language and voice we improve our ability to influence. See Chapter Seven, "Building Rapport."
- *Language:* There are distinct ways people use language to frame and express ideas. By understanding our own language preferences and those of donors, we can become more effective influencers. See Chapter Eight, "Speaking the Language of Influence."

- *Perception*: Everyone perceives the world from a different point of view—in fact from three different points of view. Reframing your proposal to match the donor's point of view can make a massive impact on the effectiveness of your ask. See Chapter Nine, "Understanding Their Point of View."

Persistence

To be a successful influencer you need to know when to keep going with a course of action—and when to change and adapt. *Persistence* involves developing the ability to demonstrate this intelligent flexibility.

For advice on how to use questions more precisely and effectively, see Chapter Ten, "Helping Donors Say 'Yes.'" To deal with the many variations of "No"—nine in total—try Chapter Eleven, "Dealing with Objections."

You might also need help when you feel low energy and disheartened. Chapter Six, "Building Self-Confidence," demonstrates the techniques that top athletes—and now you—can use to access a more positive and empowering mental state.

More Help

We've included various appendices with more detailed examples, such as Appendix B, "Using Richer Language." And we've introduced some additional material that may be useful if you find you have to influence an audience through a formal presentation (many people's worst nightmare). See Appendix D, "Influencing in a Group," for ideas on this.

Fundraising and Beyond

Most of what we cover in this book is about influence in fundraising. That means, obviously, it's a lot about how to ask for money and resources in both one-to-one and one-to-many situations. But fundraisers don't *just* ask for money. And because of that, we also explore other areas, such as how to persuade your board to invest in your ideas, how to engage a powerful advocate to speak for your cause, and how to motivate your team when their confidence is low.

Whether you need it only for fundraising or have a wider remit, influence is not an easy skill to acquire, so within the 5Ps we offer you concrete help to

- Shape your key ideas into effective messages
- Decide what action you want the person you are influencing to take
- Organize yourself and your thinking to secure that action
- Appreciate the differences in how people think and make decisions
- Measure interim successes as you develop a relationship with a donor
- Anticipate barriers, concerns, and objections to your ideas
- Build up your confidence after a series of setbacks or "No's"
- Build up the confidence or ability of inexperienced colleagues
- Learn from failure—and integrate that learning into future activities

Enjoy the influence journey.

INFLUENCE—WHAT IT IS AND WHY YOU NEED IT IN YOUR FUNDRAISING

Influence is a special kind of communication skill you probably already have. But it's a skill that you can, and must, improve to be the outstanding fundraiser your cause needs.

In this chapter we'll

- Explore how you and your improved communication can be critical to your organization's success
- Explain why high-level influence skills are particularly relevant and important to fundraisers and fundraising *now*

Our straightforward definition will help you understand exactly what influence is and what its key elements are. Arising from this definition are three implications. We identify how, if you work through these implications, you'll have *long-term* rather than *short-term* payoffs.

Finally, we help you understand the two main reasons why attempts at fundraising influence so often fail—and how our tried-and-tested 5Ps framework can help.

You Are the Success Secret!

Here are some typical fundraising challenges you might identify with. You're a committed, intelligent fundraiser working hard to secure resources for your organization and its important work. You accept the reality that you don't have the biggest marketing budget, or the most-recognized brand, or the best donor list, or the best board, or maybe even the "easiest-to-explain" cause. But you also accept that there's no point in complaining about the unfairness of it all—and you recognize that you have to raise funds in competition with organizations that may have those budgets, brands, donors, boards, and causes.

So if the question is, "How can I succeed in the competition for funds and what's my organization's success secret?" we believe the answer is *you*. Specifically, it's your ability to communicate your cause in a way that persuades donors and others to take action and offer you support. The competitive edge is your *ability to influence*. This book is about developing and improving that competitive edge so that you become a powerful and effective influencer.

Why Influence *Now?*

You could argue that fundraising has always been about influence. And in many ways that's true. But there are three pressing reasons why influence is a more important skill than it has ever been:

- First, today's donors and supporters are more sophisticated and demanding. So our grasp of techniques for persuasion also needs to be more sophisticated and targeted. It's not enough anymore just to ask people to help "the poor" or "the sick," or "the lame." Today's donors want to feel they are making informed choices and definite impacts, which means they demand better communication. But they don't necessarily want *more* information. They want it faster and in a way that they can readily understand. That puts extra pressure on us to deliver. *Influence skills can help us provide information to donors in a targeted and appropriate way to secure the result we need.*

- Second, we're all aware of the *negative* publicity certain types of mass fundraising are getting—wasteful direct mail, intrusive telephone fundraising, and spam-like e-mail and viral approaches are all attracting significant criticism. (Whoever thought *viral* marketing was a good name? Since when have viruses been thought of as something good?) As donors we don't want to feel we're part of a mass-marketing initiative. We want to feel special and important. So we like communications that are obviously about us and involve and engage us—but not in a way that just looks like a search-and-replace-key-field-in-a-database. Increasingly, there's a higher value placed on one-to-one and person-to-person contact, or at least what *feels* like such contact. *Even if we're making one of fifty phone calls we should be able to change and adapt a basic message, using influence skills, to make the individuals we're contacting feel important and valued.*

- Third, influence skills can help you engage an exceptional individual donor in a way that enables him or her to make a transformational gift to your cause. The reality is there are now more wealthy people in the world than there have ever been.[1] And the great news for fundraisers is that more of these wealthy people are philanthropic. Okay, we won't all meet the megagivers like Bill Gates, Ingvar Kamprad, Mo Ibrahim, Tom Hunter, or Carlos Slim at the dinner table. (If you only recognize Bill in this list, try Googling the others. Wealth and philanthropy are worldwide phenomena.) But we can and do meet people all the time who could make an exceptional gift. If you are introduced to potential high-value donors—whether it's Ingvar Kamprad or a local furniture store owner who wants to "give something back"—they'll want to deal with you one-to-one. *It's in these one-to-one very-high-payoff situations that you'll also need access to influence skills to engage and enthuse the megadonor.*

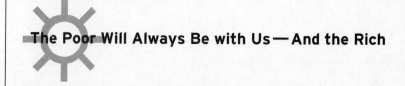

The Poor Will Always Be with Us—And the Rich

The U.S. Council on Foundations' projections are that we'll witness no less than $41 trillion in asset transfer by the middle of this century in the United States. At least

$6 trillion of this will be for charitable giving. One result is that upward of $300 billion will be available in annual foundation giving alone.

The implication for fundraisers worldwide is that there are increasing opportunities for fundraising for exceptional gifts.

(Statistics taken from a speech by Steve Gunderson—the Council's president—presented at the annual conference of the National Association of State Charity Officials (NASCO), October 2006.)

Defining Influence

So we know why we might want to influence. But before we explore *how* we influence we need to define *what influencing is*. There are a number of definitions. Our own definition—which has proved useful to clients and others we've worked with—is shown in Figure 1.1.

As you can see from the notes accompanying the main definition, simple doesn't mean simplistic. The key ideas in this definition will become important later in the book as you develop your understanding of influence. Let's look at them in more detail.

Figure 1.1 Definition of Influencing

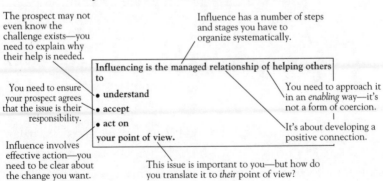

The prospect may not even know the challenge exists—you need to explain why their help is needed.

Influence has a number of steps and stages you have to organize systematically.

You need to ensure your prospect agrees that the issue is their responsibility.

You need to approach it in an *enabling* way—it's not a form of coercion.

It's about developing a positive connection.

Influence involves effective action—you need to be clear about the change you want.

This issue is important to you—but how do you translate it to *their* point of view?

Influencing is the managed relationship of helping others to
- understand
- accept
- act on

your point of view.

- *Managed relationship:* To achieve a specific outcome with an individual or group, you need to be clear on the result you want *and* have a flexible plan about how to achieve it. The book explores how to develop a specific kind of relationship.

- *Helping others:* Influence is different from negotiation[2] or coercion.[3] In influence you're trying to help someone change their mind or to come around to your point of view. Your prospect or donor should never feel manipulated. Much of the book stresses the different ways you can help people to *choose* to change their minds.

- *Understand, accept, and act:* Successful influence has to have these three elements. We want people to really *know* what the challenge is, *agree* that they have a responsibility to tackle it, and finally *do* something concrete. We don't want them just to think about it! The book emphasizes the importance of *action*—especially when the first response you get is a "No."

- *Points of view:* Throughout the book we reinforce a key issue—the way we see the world or feel about issues may not be the same for others. The really skillful influencer begins by being curious about people and framing ideas in a way that will help individuals or groups change their minds. We offer you ways to gain that skill.

Try to keep this definition, and the elements embedded in it, in your mind as you work through the book.

Why We Sometimes Can't Influence

Why do so many fundraisers go wrong in their attempts to influence? In our experience there are two common challenges.

The first is that there's a lot of *mechanistic thinking and advice about fundraising*—an emphasis on the one "right" way to write a case; or specific, almost ritual, sequences of "moves" management to engage donors; or certainty on the five key questions to ask at meetings; or even the ten "power" words "guaranteed" to close the donation deal.

Much of this approach is drawn from old-fashioned sales techniques that, although not necessarily bad in themselves, are often crudely applied as though donors were some kind of lab rats. The reality is that much of this approach just doesn't work any more—contemporary donors and supporters are more sophisticated and demanding in what messages they accept or reject.

The second is that *many fundraisers make incorrect or inappropriate assumptions about the beliefs and behaviors of others.* This then leads those fundraisers to draw the wrong conclusion about how the donor will respond to a specific technique or approach. ("I was sure she'd be moved by the photos—how could anyone not be? Why then didn't she make a donation?" Our misguided fundraiser assumes that *because a donor is socially concerned, she'll want to support their cause, and the photos will trigger this response.*)

Other examples of this "assumption-laden" thinking we've heard include the following:

- "I know you're an older person and concerned about the environment. We're an environmental charity, so please remember us in your will."
- "I know you care about young people and their education. We work with children with behavioral problems. Your $10 can help stop children from missing school."

Our experience is that fundraisers approach influence this way because they don't have the tools to adapt their own thinking and frame it in a way that is useful to others. The donor often says "No" *because* the fundraiser's "obvious" logic, sadly, isn't always theirs. This book is designed to help you as a fundraiser to understand *why* people don't always act "logically" and to show you how to take donors through the influence process successfully. That way you get the behavior or action that you're looking for—you achieve *influence*.

People Are "Messy"—So Is Influence

There isn't an easy approach to influence in fundraising or any other type of influence. Our experience is that it's complex and messy—largely because the human race is complex and messy. Unlike computers, people are not always predictable. Some donors, in fact, can appear downright "weird" to us. (The assumption is always that *we* are normal.) Their unpredictability is what makes our relationships with donors, and people in general, fun and passionate—and frustrating and puzzling. And because relationships in general are like that, the influence process is also fun and passionate—and frustrating and puzzling. As a result of our experience, we felt we needed an influence model that reflected this "messy" reality.

Note that we're not saying you should bombard a prospective donor with every technique in this book until you find one that works or they give in. We *are* saying that you need to plan your process carefully and build flexibility into it to deal with the "messiness" that will be inherent. It *is* a relationship after all.

Use the 5Ps Framework—But Use It All!

We've written this book from the vantage point of having used the 5Ps framework with individuals from many leading nonprofit organizations on both sides of the Atlantic. As a result, we can point to a significant body of success for this approach. If you use the framework—and use it systematically—we're confident that you too will be more successful, both in winning people over to your cause and in obtaining bigger and more donations.

There's just one proviso in our confidence. You need to take the time to work through the *whole* framework. You might be tempted to skip the foundations and dive ahead to the exciting and clever psychological and interpersonal techniques. There's lots of interesting and challenging material there. But it only works if you have a solid underpinning on which to base it.

Finally, with power comes some ethical considerations. The skills and techniques we share here *are* powerful. They build, as we've said, on natural processes and aspects of human relationships. They have been used by successful and ethical fundraisers in the past. And we'd like *you* to carry on using them in that spirit. We ask only that you consistently ensure you follow two rules.

- *Use these techniques where they fit with your values.*

Persuading your elderly aunt to loan you more money than she can really afford might be in your interests but probably doesn't fit with your values. Likewise, you need to judge which techniques fit with your values in fundraising terms.

- *Use these techniques with consideration for the donor's values.*

A key part of ethics and stewardship is to consider the interests of the other person—donor, colleague, and volunteer. If you feel like you're manipulating someone, then you probably are. So stop whatever you're doing.

Summary

Fundraising can seem unfair if you work for a smaller, less well-resourced, less well-known or harder-to-sell cause. The bad news is that fundraising *is* unfair. But there is good news too: you have the potential to be your organization's single biggest competitive advantage. And by improving your influence skills you can become a fabulous advantage.

Influence has always been an essential part of fundraising, but now there are pressing reasons to improve your skills. These include the negative publicity given to some mass-marketing techniques, the need to respond to the sophistication and demands of donors, and finally the growth in the number of individuals who can make a significant gift if approached sensitively.

You'll be most effective if you have a real understanding of what influence is and how it works. A key proposition at the center of our approach is that other people don't necessarily share your way of thinking or making decisions. This might have to do with values, or communication styles, or psychology, or age, or culture. To be successful you need to be able both to recognize differences and to be flexible in adapting to them.

Successful influence is not about the simplistic and mechanistic "moves management" approach endorsed by some agencies and consultants. Nor is it any longer good enough to rely on the old-fashioned "just write a good case statement and share it" school of philanthropic purity. Although these approaches sometimes work *despite* themselves, if your cause is important we believe you should use the best techniques you can.

Influence—and especially the use of sophisticated psychological techniques—involves ethical considerations. These should form part of your stewardship commitment.

At its best, fundraising influence should be about a *win-win-win*:

Win: You secure the help and resources you need.

Win: The donor feels they're engaged and contributing.

Win: Your beneficiaries or cause get the result they need.

In the next chapter we begin to explore in real depth the =mc 5Ps framework. This will guide you through influence situations. It will help you shape your message, identify likely challenges, and establish the key action that's needed. The 5Ps of Influence are

1. Passion: identifying what you want and why it's important
2. Proposal: shaping your idea in a way that's compelling

3. Preparation: organizing your ideas and thinking

4. Persuasion: using psychology to frame your influence messages

5. Persistence: dealing with challenges and objections

Chapter Two explores how to adopt the first of these stages—to shape your ideas, your *passion*—in a purposeful and practical way.

Notes

1. Philanthropy is even a hot media topic, if not quite the new rock and roll. In 2006 *Time* magazine honored Bill and Melinda Gates as "People of the Year." In the same year *The Economist* twice featured philanthropy on its cover, and *Fortune* magazine had a cover with former president Clinton and the words, "The Power of Philanthropy."

2. Usually in negotiation both sides have to compromise on something—such as the price of a service—to achieve a result. If you can't reach a compromise then the negotiation fails.

3. You're not trying to coerce someone when you influence—they have to *choose* to support you.

Part One

Passion

... to the source. It also ensures that you don't breath in ...

2

FOCUSING YOUR
PASSION—INTELLIGENTLY

The starting point for influence in a nonprofit setting should be a personal drive to achieve some wider social good. To be an *outstandingly successful* influencer you need to have a real desire—a *Passion*—for that change. This drive will sustain you when you encounter challenges. At the same time, as a practical fundraiser, you know that passion has to lead to a concrete, specific financial result.

In this chapter we concentrate on the importance of *framing and organizing* your passion or personal motivation to help you achieve the outcome you want. This ensures that you can express, but aren't overwhelmed by, your own passion or emotional commitment to the cause. It also ensures that you don't begin by assuming that other people will immediately share your passion.

We focus on two elements of success:

- First, we help you check the level of your *emotional engagement* with your cause, especially making sure you're not using "passion-killing" language. As part of this, we introduce you to a quick and effective way to create a thirty-second fundraising elevator pitch.
- Second, we help you achieve a balanced approach to sharing your passion with others whom you want to influence, using Daniel Goleman's well-established *emotional intelligence* model.

Together these elements form a key component of the first cog in the 5Ps framework: passion. With them in place you're on the road to achieving your ambition of effective influencing for outstanding fundraising results.

Successful Influencers—Focusing and Sharing Passion

For almost fifteen years we've worked with and studied successful influencers. We've seen a range of approaches work and witnessed some outstanding examples of individuals actively engaging others in different ways. These examples include Kate Gilmore, deputy secretary general of Amnesty International, "selling" a challenging change of direction to her tough, analytic, twelve-person board using a series of brilliant PowerPoint presentations over three days.[1] Another is Giles Pegram, director of fundraising for the National Society for the Prevention of Cruelty to Children (NSPCC), taking just fifteen minutes to inspire a thousand people at a conference with the story of the *Full Stop* campaign.[2]

In addition, we've studied outside the nonprofit world, assessing the approaches used by leading politicians, religious leaders, and business figures. We've noted when they succeeded in getting their message heard and analyzed how they did it. Our conclusion is that there is no single "best" approach. But one common characteristic of successful influencers—whatever their styles—is that they all seem to have a clear personal motivation—a *passion*. Not only that, they've shaped and refined their passion to have the greatest impact—greatest *influence*—on their audiences.

The range of sophisticated techniques and approaches in this book will make a significant difference in your ability to influence effectively. But even *excellent* technique is not enough on its own. *You* are the most important resource your organization has when it comes to influence. And if you don't believe *passionately* in the cause for which you are raising money, or if you can't focus and share that passion, you won't be a truly effective influencer.

From both our own experience and the research we carried out, we believe you'll succeed in your ambition to *actively engage* donors and supporters if you are able to balance two characteristics:

- Emotional engagement
- Emotional intelligence

Emotional Engagement

The starting point for your motivation is your emotional engagement with the cause. This is the fuel that

- Inspires you to greater creativity and imagination when you're working to influence someone
- Gives you the perseverance you need when things get tough and you're knocked back
- Prompts you to discipline and organize your thinking and feelings in order to learn and apply the techniques explored here

It's difficult to keep trying to influence people sometimes. This is especially true if your cause is "unpopular" or unattractive and you experience a lot of rejection, or seem to spend your whole time having to overcome prejudice or ignorance. (Unpopular or unattractive can mean a range of things, from abortion rights in parts of the United States to contemporary atonal music concerts in a working-class estate in the United Kingdom.)

To carry on in the face of obstacles and outright rejection, you need access to the emotional energy that comes from real engagement. It's your *emotional engagement*—your commitment to the cause—that will make you keep trying different approaches until you get a result. It won't necessarily mean a 24/7, high-energy, flushed-face rushing around (there's only so much one body can take). Emotional engagement can, in fact, be quiet, low-key, and purposeful. But whether it's high energy or quiet it needs to show in the things you say and do.

A Quiet Influencer

One of our influencing heroes is Giles Pegram, for twenty-five years the legendary director of fundraising at the United Kingdom's NSPCC (National Society for the Prevention of Cruelty to Children), and part of the leadership team that created the inspirational *Full Stop* campaign.

Giles is essentially a quiet man. He doesn't wave his arms around. He speaks softly and with gentle humor. He chooses his words carefully. So his emotional engagement is not of the florid kind. But he has a marvelous way of winning people over to his cause. One way he does this is through a refrain he uses when he's selling a difficult idea. He finishes with, "Think. What will this mean for children?" So when he asks a donor to make a significant step-up gift, he asks the donor to consider "what your contribution will mean for children." And when he asks his colleagues to undertake a challenging restructure, he acknowledges the pain and difficulty and then asks them to reflect on "what this new structure will mean for children."

People who work with the NSPCC—whether as volunteers or staff—are bound together by their concern for children. When Giles uses his "What will it mean?" refrain it is both an emotional touchstone and an intellectual benchmark. He's asking his colleagues to live up to a *quiet, reflective, shared passion*.

(If you've read our book *Breakthrough Thinking*, Jossey-Bass 2002, you'll know how much we admire *Full Stop*. This hugely ambitious and successful campaign, designed to "end cruelty to children," reinvented many of the "rules" of major volunteer-led campaigns.)

Communicate with Yourself

To check your current level of engagement with your cause, try this test on yourself. Stand up and say your organization's mission out loud, as if explaining to someone what it is you do. Can you remember it? Assuming you can, as you say the mission what comes to mind? What images does it conjure? How does it make you feel? If your response is "Nothing" or "Very little," then our advice is to get a new mission. Or get a new job. Or learn to communicate better with *yourself* by reengaging with your organization's mission and the passion it *should* generate.

To ensure that *you and your team* are engaged with your work, try

- Thinking back to the first thing that attracted you to work for your current organization—was it an experience, or the job advertisement, or a meeting?
- Making a list of reasons why you work for the organization you're influencing and fundraising on behalf of.
- Sharing your lists and comparing notes as a way of exploring the core values that bind you.

Talk Passionately

The most common form of communication is language. Unfortunately, charities, nonprofits, or NGOs (nongovernmental organizations) can be worse than government bureaucrats for "jargon"—lifeless and impenetrable, often technical language.

If we use jargon, we're in danger of both dampening our own passion and failing to light a spark in other people. Plutarch said, "The mind is a fire to be ignited, not a vessel to be filled." But how many charities set out to *ignite* people in the way they talk about their cause? To capture their interest and imagination with sizzle? More often charities and those who work for them seem to speak a bizarre, convoluted language that leaves people confused or—worse still—bored. That language can also help kill *our* passion.

Here are some real examples of such "lifeless" language killing the passion behind hugely important drives to improve the lives of the poorest people on the planet. We got them from individuals working in the organizations. Note that the organizations that produced these pieces of language do *excellent* work. But how engaged will people be from outside the organizations if this is what they hear? And if the starting point for passion should always be simple and direct communication—firelighting, not fact filling—how do these compare?

- "Perinatal mortality through maternal HIV transmission is 35%." (UNAIDS—the United Nations agency charged with dealing with the HIV/AIDS pandemic.)
- "Almost 25% of the world's under-12s are malnourished." (UNICEF—another UN agency, charged with protecting the interests of the world's children.)
- "Primary education is denied to 85% of female children in the developing world." (Save the Children Alliance—the Alliance is the international network of agencies with a goal to ensure all children receive at least a basic education.)

It seems unlikely that any of these statements has lit a fire for social justice in you or in anyone else. Worse still, we're not sure that many people would be completely clear about what they actually mean. We think the very smart and very committed people who wrote those things were trying to say something along the lines of the following:

- "One in three babies born to mothers who are HIV positive die within six months if the illness is passed on at birth."
- "One in four children under twelve goes to bed hungry every night—that's almost three million children in sub-Saharan Africa alone."
- "More than four out of five girls in the developing world are denied the chance to learn basic skills such as reading and writing."

Put the information across in straightforward language, and *other* people will certainly understand what it is you are saying.

As important, when you speak simply and clearly about critical issues *your* passion should be fired—and if *your* passion is fired, there's a much stronger chance your donor's will be. Begin with passion—and then use the ideas and techniques in the book to *focus and frame your passion.*

Your Elevator Pitch

You're probably familiar with the *elevator pitch* idea. The pure version may be Hollywood apocrypha, but broadly this is the way it goes. As a budding film director keen to have your film made, you fix it so that you get into the elevator with the big producer on the first floor. The producer is heading for his office on the seventh floor. So you have six floors—or thirty seconds—in which to "sell" your idea. Apocrypha or not, we think the discipline of the elevator pitch is a good one, and we often spend time coaching fundraisers or even CEOs to help them create their own.

Here's the framework we use. Every elevator pitch should have three elements: *think, feel,* and *do.* These elements are designed to help shape your thinking and to answer some very specific questions. See Table 2.1 for how this works.

Table 2.1 Elevator Pitch Framework, Example One

Element	Questions	Example (chair of the development committee speaking to the board)
Think	What is it you want your audience *to know or understand* as a result of this communication?	"We have recently heard that donor X will match any gift we can secure from a company up to $1 million."
Feel	What *emotion* do you want them to have as they receive the communication. (This could be excitement, concern, uncertainty, or so on. But it should be a specific emotion.)	"This is great news, and I'm sure you share my excitement about the possibilities it creates for us to finish the capital appeal."
Do	What specific action do you want the listener(s) to take as a result of this message?	"I need you to call all your corporate contacts and ask them to commit any funds they can in the next six months."

Of course if you change the audience and the purpose you can use the same formula to create a very different kind of impact (see Table 2.2).

Next time you have to present a message to a key audience in a quick and insightful way, try using the "Think, Feel, Do" formula. That way you can make sure you're clear about the outcome you want in terms of the core information in your message and the emotional response you expect it to stimulate. That should then lead you to specific action you need.

Note that you *reverse* the order when you're *preparing* your elevator pitch:

1. Begin with the people that you want to influence—individual or group—and be clear on exactly what *action* you want them to take.

Table 2.2 Elevator Pitch Framework, Example Two

Element	Example (development director speaking to a potential major donor)
Think	"Without a gift of $.5 million in the next six weeks the theater workshop will close. The five hundred underprivileged children who attend the weekly drama classes will be denied access to the creative outlet that they have had for almost five years."
Feel	"I'm really distressed about the idea of having to break that news. And I'm sure that, like me, you would feel ashamed if a town of this size had no creative arts opportunity for children aged five to ten."
Do	"I'd like you to consider shortening the timescale we've discussed for the gift you've agreed to make."

2. Imagine the *emotion* or *feeling* in those people (not you!) that is most likely to move them to take that action.

3. Finally, select and shape the *information* or data that you think is most likely to create that emotion—if people only knew it.

Emotional Intelligence

Managing your emotion is as important as having emotions. If you simply emote, donors or others may not identify with the feeling you're having or may simply regard you as passionate but flaky. *You* may feel motivated, but they won't.

So you need emotional intelligence (EI) to manage your passion. The term *EI* was popularized by Daniel Goleman in his book *Emotional Intelligence* (Bantam, 1997), although the basic concept had been around for some time before this. Essentially he describes it as the ability to successfully manage your internal and external relationships. In this context, *internal* means the security and confidence you have about yourself, your needs, your values, and your beliefs. And *external* means the way in which you interact and engage effectively with others in social and professional settings. This combination of internal and external emotional management helps you achieve more and is critical to successful influence.[3]

According to Goleman, there are five dimensions to EI. We're not going to go into these in detail. But in order to get the most out of the other skills and techniques we explore in this book, you'll need to know about and have access to the dimensions:

- Self-awareness
- Self-regulation
- Motivation
- Empathy
- Social skills

Table 2.3 shows what each of these is and how they are relevant to you in a fundraising influence setting.

EI skills and abilities are fundamental to success in a range of settings—at work and in your personal life, as well as in fundraising influence. The EI model's first three elements—self-awareness, self-regulation, and motivation—will help you to manage *your* passion or commitment. The second cluster will help you to understand others and *their* passions, concerns, and motivations.

Our experience confirms that emotionally intelligent fundraisers and influencers are simply more successful. Giles Pegram's emotionally intelligent appeal is to a *shared* passion, "What will it mean for children?"

Developing EI Skills in Others

As well as developing your *own* EI skills it's useful to be able to spot or develop these skills in *others*. You can then include these people in your influence approach.

Table 2.3 Five Dimensions of Emotional Intelligence

Dimension	Definition	Influencing Implication
Self-awareness	The ability to recognize and understand our moods, emotions, and drives. Being realistic in our assessment of ourselves and our abilities.	Understanding what motivates or excites you about the cause Sensing *why* you feel uncomfortable or angry when provoked—perhaps by a donor's unreasonable request for a report-back over a weekend Being clear about what you want from a situation and what the benefits might be
Self-regulation	The ability to control or redirect unhelpful impulses and moods, and the tendency to suspend judgement and to think before acting.	Staying calm when there's a crisis—for example, the caterer fails to turn up for your cultivation event Not lashing out when attacked or criticized for a controversial or difficult decision Not having mood swings in front of the development team when things go better, or less well
Motivation	Using our deepest preferences and drivers to move us to take the initiative toward our goals—and the ability to persevere.	Being clear about your values and sticking to them—perhaps challenging a donor even though this risks losing the gift or perhaps your job Staying connected emotionally to your cause over a sustained period of time Not losing heart when things don't go well—and being able to support colleagues or volunteers when they feel anxious

(continued)

Table 2.3 (continued)

Dimension	Definition	Influencing Implication
Empathy	The ability to recognize what others are feeling and see their perspective, and skills in treating them according to their needs and concerns.	Being "fair" and balanced in your assessment of others—maybe understanding why a donor might reasonably say "No" Accurately understanding how others might feel in a given situation Expressing *appropriate* emotions and feelings to others
Social skills	The ability to "read" social situations—and skills in starting, managing, and building on relationships with individuals and groups.	Recognizing and managing a group dynamic, such as a volunteer board or team meeting Choosing the "right" kind of relationship to have with someone—balancing "friendliness" with your professional relationship Successfully maintaining friendships and professional relationships over time

One especially useful group of people to have access to when you're trying to influence are called *connectors*. These are people with lots of friends and associates—which means they are strong on the second cluster of EI skills. Malcolm Gladwell coined the word *connectors* in his seminal book *The Tipping Point* (Little Brown, 2000). In the book he explains that some individuals have both extensive social connections *and* great social power. They usually know people across an array of social, cultural, professional, and financial circles. If you ask them, "Do you know anyone I can stay with in L.A.?" the connector will offer you a choice of ten people, all of whom they're sure would offer you a bed because he or she is a personal friend.

Their extraordinary networks mean a connector can be enormously useful in expanding the scope of a fundraiser's influence project. A key reason for this is because most people are much more likely to do something if asked by a friend or close associate.

Here's an example. Bernard recently attended a conference run by the Association of Lutheran Development Executives in Baltimore. He was introduced, over dinner, to Pastor Robert Knott, who organizes an outstandingly successful door-to-door fundraising collection week in the Midwest. Pastor Knott is a shy man, and he's only one person, so he uses connectors to help him achieve his result and support the ministry. In particular, the pastor is immensely proud of one specific connector-parishioner who organizes and runs a short program that he reckons makes the whole scheme work.

Bernard later met Pastor Knott's connector—a redoubtable sixty-year-old widow, Roberta, and she told him the secrets of her success.

First she invited fellow Lutherans she knew from throughout the city to come to a meeting—selling it as a social gathering. At the meeting she asked them to support the work of the parish by acting as collectors in their own neighborhoods. She then delivered a concise briefing and training that took the form of six simple guidelines. We think they're a superb distillation of the principles of emotional intelligence in action. Here are "Roberta's Rules" for organizing a world-class collection.

- Arrange to personally drop off the envelopes at a time when people are most likely to be at home so you can meet them—don't just put the envelope in the mailbox.

- When you ring the doorbell and they answer, explain first that you are a neighbor if you don't directly know them. Mention, if you have, that you have seen them in the street or supermarket. Or, apologize that you haven't.

- Notice and mention something positive about the decor on the outside of the house. Compliment them on their yard if they have one. And mention it's great that people around here take pride in such things.

- Explain what you're doing and emphasize it's a community or parish activity run by local volunteers to help others.

- Hand them the envelope and ask for a donation. Don't say "however small." Mention that this is a big challenge, and you're hoping that this neighborhood or parish will be a top contributor as in previous years.

- Explain that you'll be back tomorrow at about the same time, if that's okay, to collect the envelope. Or if not, ask when would be a good time to come back. And make sure you stick to that arrangement. Remember, this person is now your friend!

EI often sounds like common sense. And much of it is. If you're looking to achieve influence, make sure you don't just rely on your own talents and abilities. Find others—especially connectors—and ask them to help extend your sphere of influence.

Summary

Fundraising needs passion. You'll never succeed without personal passion to drive you, and to help you to overcome the challenges that trying to influence others brings. But you need to be able to properly focus and channel your passion if you're going to communicate it and use it to real effect.

There are two elements to focusing your passion—*emotional engagement* and *emotional intelligence*.

High levels of *emotional engagement* are essential. You need to feel *engaged* in your cause and communicate that engagement even if you've been involved in it for years. More than that you need to openly demonstrate that you share your organization's beliefs and values. If you don't do this, how can you possibly hope to engage a donor at anything more than a superficial level?

Passion doesn't mean wild emotion—it can be most powerful when it's quiet and restrained.

A starting point to achieve that focused intensity is to avoid the use of passion-quenching language so common in many charity missions and causes.

To share your engagement try the discipline of an "elevator pitch"—can you shape and communicate your passion in a coherent way in thirty seconds or less? Use the "Think, Feel, Do" formula to ensure that your message is organized effectively. When you're *shaping* your pitch, you need to begin with the action you want others to take, *then* choose the emotion that is most likely to drive that action, and *finally* select the information that will help generate that emotion in the donor.

The second characteristic of effective fundraising passion is *emotional intelligence*. EI provides a combination of internal and external emotional management techniques that help you to shape and present your feelings to others *and* understand their response.

According to Daniel Goleman, the EI guru, there are five key dimensions you need to access to achieve high levels of emotional intelligence:

- Self-awareness: understanding what you want
- Self-regulation: controlling your feelings
- Motivation: having the energy and commitment to do something
- Empathy: understanding how others feel
- Social skills: being able to get on with others

Working through these five dimensions and assessing your competence in each will give you a more rounded view of yourself and your own passion. And that will help you to share that passion more easily using the techniques in the subsequent chapters.

Finally, being *personally* emotionally intelligent may not be enough to achieve the fundraising result you want. Look to use your influencing skills to recruit and involve other people with high EI in your staff and volunteer teams. These people can be a huge asset.

And if you need to organize people for a mass event, find and use what Malcolm Gladwell calls *connectors*—individuals able to draw in large numbers to assist. You can also help people to *become* connectors using "Roberta's Rules."

Notes

1. Kate Gilmore and her colleague Irene Khan are the two most significant figures in the world of defending human rights. Working together they have helped transform the work of Amnesty International in the last five years, including creating the successful campaign to reduce violence against women worldwide.

2. The NSPCC (National Society for the Prevention of Cruelty to Children) ran the breakthrough *Full Stop* campaign in the United Kingdom. Its challenging overall goal was "to end child abuse in a generation." The accompanying fundraising appeal was the largest volunteer donor appeal of its kind in Europe at that time. It raised $500 million for a difficult-to-sell-and-explain issue using a number of groundbreaking approaches to achieve its challenging target. We use the appeal as an example throughout the book.

3. There's a significant body of work published by the Center for Applied Emotional Intelligence that suggests a high level of EI is a key factor in success. For the past four years (2005–2008) we have been running a survey among high-achieving fundraisers at the Association of Fundraising Professionals' annual international conference. To date, successful fundraisers (those with fifteen or more years of experience) score some 10 to 14 percent higher than average on the EI scale.

3

UNDERSTANDING DONOR MOTIVATIONS

The desire to change or improve things for some wider social good is not the exclusive gift of people who work in charities or nonprofits. Donors, volunteers, and even corporations also want to do good—they too have their passion. (We also need to accept that people sometimes do good things for reasons that aren't necessarily about altruism, but rather to a meet personal desire or ambition.)

To be successful influencers we have to learn to understand and tap into these different donor motivations.

Specifically in this chapter we focus on

- The importance of understanding what donor motivations are and how they can vary from person to person and from situation to situation.
- The idea of what are technically called "hygiene" factors—a concept from social psychology that explains why many influencers fail early on, before they've even had a chance to share their passion.
- The distinction between three often-confused motivation elements—*features*, *benefits*, and *motivators*. It's important to distinguish these elements, especially when you're working with commercial sponsors.

Motivation—The Driver to Action

Understanding someone else's feelings and motivations—their *passion*—is essential to bringing them on board with your proposal. The empathy and social skills elements of the EI model explored in Chapter Two are invaluable in helping you do this.

29

Because this book is about influencing skills for fundraisers, we're focusing mostly on *fundraising* situations and on *donor* motivations—whether you're trying to influence an individual, a foundation, or a company. But the principles we explore here are also relevant to non-fundraising situations, from convincing your staff to work differently to persuading your partner to agree with your idea for a holiday.

Let's begin by defining what's meant by a *motivation*—our definition is *an internal or external driver that makes an individual start or stop an action.* There are a couple of key elements here:

- *Internal or external:* People can change because of something *inside* them—their values, beliefs, or sense of self. Alternatively, they can change because of something *external* to them—to impress, to gain advancement, or because a hero or heroine asks, and so on. *Both sources of motivation are valid and both fit in with the major theories of human motivation, from Maslow's hierarchy of need to Vroom's expectancy theory.*

- *Start or stop action:* People may also be motivated to *start* something—donate a gift, recruit a colleague, make an introduction. Alternatively, they may be motivated to *stop* something—cease disruptive behavior in board meetings, or even give up a hobby or holiday to devote more time to the cause, and so on. The challenge is to create a motivator strong enough to create action.

If you're not sure what you're trying to motivate someone *to do* (or stop doing) you'll have problems in achieving a successful outcome. Worst of all you may end up motivating them to do the wrong thing. Let's assume at the moment that you *are* clear on the outcome you want. But if you need help, see Chapter Five, "Shaping Outcomes," for more on this.

Motivation Misconceptions

We need to dispense with one of the key misconceptions about human motivation—that person A's motivation always makes sense to person B. Not everyone is like us. So the way someone else acts—or the logic or feelings underpinning that—may appear odd to us. To be successful in influence it's essential we understand and accept this.

However, all our experience—and a significant body of academic research—confirms that *how* people will respond in certain circumstances *can be predicted*. It's this ability to notice and understand people's patterns of behavior and decision making that will help us to be excellent in influence. This still doesn't mean the motivator will itself make sense—certainly not to us and quite possibly not even to them.

Two Elements to Consider

When thinking about approaching a donor, most fundraisers begin with what "benefits" or motivators are most likely to bring the donor on board. These benefits could be spiritual, or the opportunity to gain access to someone important, or even a means to assuage guilt. However, our practical work in fundraising consultancy shows there is a step before *motivators*, especially with major donors. That step involves understanding the importance of what are called *hygiene factors*. (Sorry for the slightly strange-sounding phrase, but it is a technical term.)

The *idea* of hygiene factors comes from management guru Frederick Herzberg. Herzberg was a social psychologist who studied motivation in the context of work. After extensive research, he argued that when people are at work there are two factors at play: *hygiene* factors and *motivating* factors.[1] We've defined the very specific meanings for these terms in the following sections. A key outcome of Herzberg's research—and one that's backed up by much contemporary motivational thinking—is that hygiene factors *must* be addressed before motivators will have any positive impact. Our experience is that the same is true in fundraising influence.

Hygiene Factors

These fundamental components are about "a sense of security" or "feeling that things are fair and proper." So we expect certain elements to be present in any situation, and only notice them if they're not there. For example, having a written employment contract, or a desk, when you start a job are hygiene factors. You're not going to be excited or motivated to work harder for an employer who provides these things. You'll simply accept that these are part of a "normal" employment package. But if these components are *missing*, you feel dissatisfied or demotivated—the hygiene factors you expect to be present aren't there.

Motivating Factors

Motivators are "added value" components and are about elements such as "feeling recognized by peers" or "having a sense of personal achievement"—that is, issues that offer more than we expect to be present in any situation. For example, going back to our work illustration, being sent a note from the chief executive when you start a job might well be unexpected. You could be excited or motivated to work harder for an employer who provides such a personal touch. You see that kind of initiative as extending beyond the "expected" or "fundamental" package.

Adapting Herzberg to Fundraising and Influence

Herzberg's original work wasn't *directly* linked to influence or indeed to work with donors and fundraising, so we've taken the basic idea of hygiene factors and motivators and adapted it. Figure 3.1 shows how we use it.

Herzberg in a Fundraising Workplace

We once worked with a director of development who was puzzled as to why her team members weren't on board and motivated about the new campaign. She explained her motivational influence strategy: "I give them praise, I bring cookies into work, I seek their opinion in team meetings about the campaign—and still they don't seem engaged." We interviewed the team. "Yes," they agreed, "she does do all those things—and we like that. But we're really unhappy about the new arrangement for parking. We used to all have spaces. Now a change in the rules means some of us can get parking spaces in the morning and some can't. It's not fair." We told the director that Herzberg's advice would be that she needed to sort out this parking *hygiene* factor before her motivation approach would work.

What are the hygiene factors for your team and what are the motivators? Are they the same as for you? Does the team *share* hygiene factors and motivators? Or do team members have very individual needs?

- Donors, especially major donors, need to feel confident that their *hygiene* factors are in place (the top line off to the left) before they *consider* your cause for a donation. They need to feel safe with your cause and approach and their potential investment in it. They need an *absence of concerns*.

Figure 3.1 Donor Motivation

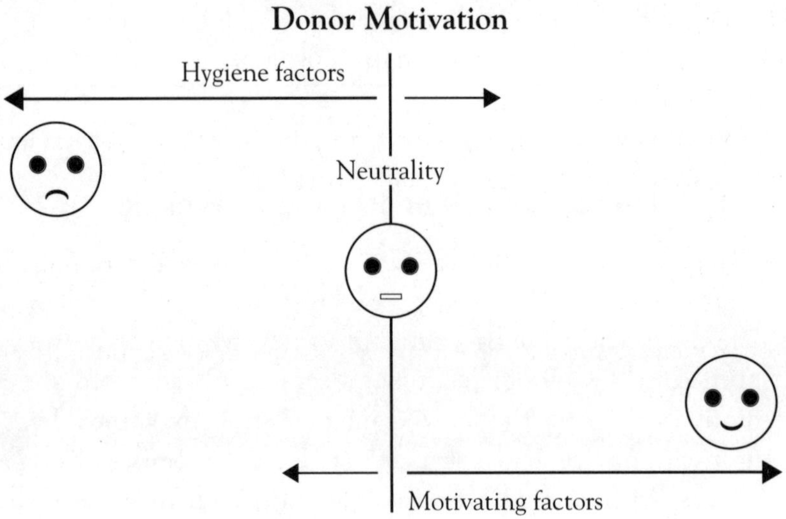

Donor Motivation

- Once there's an *absence of concerns*, you simply get *neutrality* (the vertical line in the middle of the diagram). At this point the donor doesn't have strong feelings about you either way. Here nothing much happens unless you do something extra. Absence of concerns or neutrality aren't enough to secure a donation.

- Donors then need some form of *motivation* (the bottom line off to the right) to believe in you and contribute to your cause. And they need *significant* motivation to make a *significant* donation. The further along the bottom line to the right you can move them, the better.

- If you offer motivation but there are some underlying concerns or hygiene factors that are unaddressed, then your motivational approach will not work no matter how hard you try. This means that if the donor is worried about your financial stability—*hygiene*—they probably won't make a donation to your orchestra no matter how much they love the music.

What Are *Hygiene Factors* for Donors?

Hygiene factors can vary for different people, different sectors, and different cultures. You need to consider the implications of this carefully.

Whatever they are in your context, the *purpose* of hygiene factors in fundraising is essentially threefold:

- *To provide security:* You're financially and organizationally safe.
- *To create credibility:* You have some track record and status in the field.
- *To meet expectations:* They fit with the donor's view of what is reasonable and normal

Typically for a high-value donor specific hygiene factors might include

- The fact you've got a good board
- Your attractive annual report
- Evidence of past financial probity
- An appropriate level of financial reserves
- Charity or nonprofit registration
- Other high-profile patrons
- Donor recognition systems
- A stewardship program
- A demonstrable track record of past success
- A robust business plan

Let's be clear what the implication is here. No one—well, almost no one!—will give you money *because* you have a good board or a charity registration or a good track record of past success or a stewardship program. But if you *don't* have those things they will most probably feel disinclined to support you. Hygiene factors are simply the "ticket to the party." You're likely to have to work harder than that to gain a significant donation.

Interestingly, the hygiene factors might be very specific. For some people, something as simple as correct spelling can be a hygiene factor. We've seen donors look at a proposal or a piece of promotional material and spot a typo. They then say, "If they can't bother to spellcheck, how can I trust them with my money?" Unfair? Yes. True? Sadly, also yes.

If you want to approach a company, our experience suggests that the hygiene factors might include all of the above, *plus* the following:

- High brand awareness—you're known by the customers they're interested in reaching.
- Outstanding work in your service area—you're not just good, but a leader in your field.

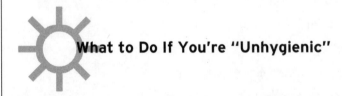

What to Do If You're "Unhygienic"

Sometimes individuals and organizations complain that having to meet hygiene factors is unfair. It's particularly challenging if your organization has only just been established—how do you create credibility?—or if you're working in a radical or experimental way—how do you provide security? In our opinion, you still need to provide at least some hygiene factors. Can you find a senior and respected figure from outside the organization to endorse your radical work? Or will an exceptionally strong business plan help address the donor's concerns on financial security?

What Are Donor *Motivators*?

Motivators are the *drivers* that encourage donors to take appropriate action—for example, to give to or join the board. There are a number of excellent books about donor motivation in general, so we don't plan to repeat that information here. It's important to say, however, that motivators do vary from person to person, and indeed from company to company or foundation to foundation (and from culture to culture).

When you've addressed the very particular hygiene factors needed by your potential donors, it's important to be just as selective with the motivators. At this point it's worth brainstorming all the possibilities as to why someone might want to support your cause. A classic list might include the following:

- A sense of affinity with others
- A sense of affinity with the cause
- A feeling of guilt
- To gain peer respect
- To gain family respect
- To gain self-respect
- To get to meet a hero or heroine
- To celebrate a success
- To celebrate an anniversary
- Personal experience of the cause
- A desire to make a difference
- A desire to "give back"
- A sense of duty based on family, business, or social role
- A dimension of faith
- A commitment to a value or belief
- A sense of anger or outrage

The rest of this book deals with how to *uncover* these motivations and even how to help donors understand or articulate their own motivations more accurately. (We're none of us always clear on why we do what we do.)

In our experience donors often have a mixture of *three or four* motivators that might encourage them to contribute. It's rarely just one, and it's never the whole list of possible motivators. A common mistake among inexperienced influencers is to "overdo" the motivators—writing them *all* into the proposition or even blurting them all out. It's much better to target an individual's key personal motivators. Think of the PIN code you need to get cash from an ATM. It has four numbers that, when used in the correct sequence, let you access your account. Work to find your donor's personal PIN code. Once you have the four keys *and* the right sequence you'll be able to unlock his or her motivation more easily. You will have found the donor's "hot buttons."

Getting the Motivator Right—Eventually

A homelessness charity in the United Kingdom thought it saw a synergy between its campaign to get homeless people off the streets of London and into safe overnight accommodation and a leading entrepreneur who had just sold his chain of shops for a significant profit. The development director sent him a letter laying out the charity's case for support in terms that were "sure" to appeal to the entrepreneur—let's call him Mr. W. We've done a précis of the appeal letter for you:

"*Dear Mr. W,*

Many people do not realize that every night two thousand people sleep rough [on the streets] in London. However,

*we know through our outreach workers that a good num-
ber of these homeless people sleep in the doorways of your former
shops. You and your staff have been very patient with this situation, despite the problems it's caused. Thank you from all of us
here, and from your doorway sleepers.*

*You may be asking yourself now, 'What has this got to
do with me? Those are no longer my shops.' A fair question.
However, I thought that, both as a businessman and a person
well-known for your social concern, you would be interested
to help put an end to a social iniquity and solve a business
challenge. . . ."*

And so it went on explaining the importance of corporate social responsibility and the long-term impact of
homeless people on the economy.

Despite the appeal's apparently "surefire" motivator—
hitting both business orientation and social conscience
—Mr. W. wrote back and said "No." The situation seemed
hopeless.

In despair the development director came to us. We
looked Mr. W. up in Who's Who. There we found he was a
devout Catholic.

Now at that time, it just so happened the president
of the charity in question was a cardinal in the Catholic
Church. The next step was simple—get the president to
write to the entrepreneur explaining why he thought it was
a matter of faith to support the needs of the homeless. This
time Mr. W. said "Yes."

The right person had made the right appeal for the right
reason. The motivator for Mr. W wasn't logical argument, or
even an argument based on socially engaged entrepreneur-
ship; it was an appeal to his Catholic duty from someone he
saw as his spiritual guide and leader.

Motivating Commercial Sponsors—The Midtown Case

Let's think about how this model might work in a specific setting—one to do with commercial sponsorship rather than individual donors.

We do a lot of work with arts and cultural organizations keen to influence companies to make an investment in their activities. In their communications with businesses these organizations nearly always put an emphasis on the high *artistic quality* of what they do—assuming that this will be a *motivator*.

Our experience suggests that artistic quality is viewed by corporate sponsors as a prerequisite for any conversation to *start*. It's a *hygiene* factor, and if the work of the organization isn't excellent the corporation will have no interest in even *discussing* a sponsorship. Hygiene factors get you in the door. It's the *motivators* that win you the business.

Midtown Center for Contemporary Arts

Look at the opening paragraphs of Figure 3.2, a (real) letter written by an arts center's corporate sponsorship manager to a potential company funder.

Notice how the manager starts quite well with the hygiene factors—building the credibility and safety of the organization. This should reassure the donor. She then lets herself down by moving on to "benefits" that are in fact *features*. (We've changed the name of the organization and the donor to save any further embarrassment.)

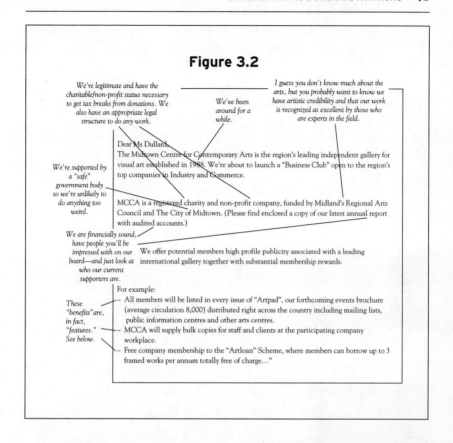

Figure 3.2

We're legitimate and have the charitable/non-profit status necessary to get tax breaks from donations. We also have an appropriate legal structure to do any work.

We've been around for a while.

I guess you don't know much about the arts, but you probably want to know we have artistic credibility and that our work is recognized as excellent by those who are experts in the field.

Dear Ms Dullard,

The Midtown Centre for Contemporary Arts is the region's leading independent gallery for visual art established in 1988. We're about to launch a "Business Club" open to the region's top companies in Industry and Commerce.

We're supported by a "safe" government body so we're unlikely to do anything too weird.

MCCA is a registered charity and non-profit company, funded by Midland's Regional Arts Council and The City of Midtown. (Please find enclosed a copy of our latest annual report with audited accounts.)

We are financially sound, have people you'll be impressed with on our board—and just look at who our current supporters are.

We offer potential members high profile publicity associated with a leading international gallery together with substantial membership rewards.

For example:

These "benefits" are, in fact, "features." See below.

– All members will be listed in every issue of "Artpad", our forthcoming events brochure (average circulation 8,000) distributed right across the country including mailing lists, public information centres and other arts centres.
– MCCA will supply bulk copies for staff and clients at the participating company workplace.
– Free company membership to the "Artloan" Scheme, where members can borrow up to 3 framed works per annum totally free of charge…"

It's not just arts and cultural organizations that fall into this trap. We found exactly the same when we were asked to advise a major U.S. east coast university on sponsorship. The university was keen to stress its excellent academic track record and how it had been established for over one hundred years. We had to remind them of all the other major academic institutions that the donor was probably talking to that also had excellent academic records. The "track record" opened the door, it didn't get a seat at the table. They had to offer more for motivation.

As part of your work with any individual donor or cluster of donors you should think carefully about what *they* might consider a hygiene factor. (Bear in mind that a hygiene factor for one cluster may put off another. For example, World Vision's faith base might be a basic requirement for some Christian donors but a disincentive for an agnostic or someone of another faith.)

Influencing Sponsors—Features, Benefits, and Motivators

Let's explore the issue of commercial sponsorship motivations in more detail here, and make a helpful distinction between three elements that are often confused—features, benefits, and motivators.

Imagine you're looking for a car. The car salesperson encourages you to buy using a combination of the following three elements:

- *Feature:* Features are the characteristics something has—for example, "This car has airbags." This is a description of *intrinsic performance qualities*—the car either does or doesn't have airbags. Essentially, if the salesperson uses this approach, he or she assumes that any buyer would be able to work out what exactly an airbag is and why it would benefit them. As a charity you may think that mentioning you have a gala evening is enough—sponsors will work out for themselves why this is of interest.

- *Benefit:* The more sophisticated salesperson might be sure to stress the specific way in which this characteristic will offer an advantage—for example, "With the airbags you'll be safe in a crash." Any product or service will have a number of benefits. And many charities will be able to offer a number of benefits to a company able to offer support. So for our gala night you might mention that the benefits could be a chance to entertain customers or to reward loyal staff.

- *Motivator:* A motivator is one of a small cluster of benefits that are important and actually spur us to action—for example, your car salesperson might say, "I understand you have children. I guess their safety is important to you. The airbags can help ensure that safety." This protection for the children might be the key motivator for a customer with a family. Persuading someone to buy your offering—whether it's a car or a proposal to fund wells providing clean water to villages in Zambia—involves more than simply presenting a list of benefits and hoping one of them hits home. As a fundraiser, you have to *preselect* the *small combination of benefits* that you believe will encourage the donor to take the action you want. At that point they are *motivators*.

So you might start with a list of twenty *features* in your sponsorship proposal that you can, with skill and practice, express as *benefits*. However, of those twenty benefits, maybe only six will be perceived by the sponsor as of any real value to his or her company. And of those six, just three are likely to be genuine, high-impact *motivators*. The skill, then, is to identify and focus on these last hot buttons.

How Does This Work in Practice?

We provide two examples of how this can work in practice—one for a corporate sponsor and the other for an individual high-value donor.

In Table 3.1, the Anytown Opera Company is trying to motivate the local CarCo to persuade them to sponsor a production of *The Marriage of Figaro*. CarCo has just set up in business and is, therefore, mostly interested in building awareness of what it has to offer among people with the disposable income to buy their mid-range to high-end cars.

Staying with Anytown Opera Company, let's try the same thing for an individual. This time, in Table 3.2, it's Ms. Smith, who is CEO of her own company. She lost her husband to heart disease twelve months ago and has thrown herself into a frenzy of philanthropy.

It's often helpful to use this layout to work out what the three levels are so that the motivators are clear.

Table 3.1 Influencing Sponsors, Example One

Feature	Benefit	Motivator	Comments
CarCo will have access to a private room before and after performances.	CarCo will be able to entertain key customers in a prestigious setting before and after performances.	???—Is there one? See comment to the right.	The challenge here is that CarCo may not have any customers yet. (They've just set up!) So while it's definitely a feature—and maybe a benefit in the future—it's *not* a motivator.
CarCo will have access to the mailing list of opera goers.	CarCo will be able to write to all of Anytown Opera's customers and introduce them to the models that CarCo carries.	CarCo can offer all of our high-value Opera Circle members a chance to attend a special event before the opera—attended by some of the performers—to introduce the company and its range of cars.	This is probably exactly what CarCo wants—the chance to meet other people who could also be potential customers.

Table 3.2 Influencing Sponsors, Example Two

Feature	Benefit	Motivator	Comments
You'll have a plaque put up in our foyer.	People will be able to see that you are a generous and sophisticated person.	???—Not necessarily a motivator.	Maybe Ms. Smith already feels generous and sophisticated —so this is a not a motivator.
You'll have a plaque put up in our foyer honoring the memory of your husband.	People will be able to see that you are a loving person.	You will feel that you have signaled how much you loved your husband—not to others so much, more to yourself.	Maybe Ms. Smith felt some guilt that when she was married she never really spent enough time with her husband.

Summary

Donor passion—motivation—is complex and inherently "messy." The starting point in influence is to accept that other people—donors included—may not share *your* passion or motivation. So you need to be curious about them and their needs and interests.

As fundraisers, we can learn a great deal from the wider world of social psychology about motivation. The work of Herzberg is especially useful and important in this. When you're thinking about your donor, consider the following:

- *Hygiene* factors that make him or her feel safe in philanthropy terms and want to work with you. This could be a range of things from a comprehensive stewardship program to a reliable and effective board of directors.

- *Motivators* that drive action—the gift or behavior change we want. These could be based on internal factors, such as self-satisfaction, or external ones, such as the chance to meet a hero or heroine.

Note that you need to make sure the hygiene factors are in place *before* the motivators can have any impact. If you try to emphasize motivators when the hygiene factors are missing you'll struggle to get the donor on board.

When thinking about commercial sponsors you might find it helpful to distinguish the three key levels of drivers to action:

- *Features*: the essential performance characteristics of something—two thousand posters will be printed for the event
- *Benefits*: the way the feature will pay off for the company—two thousand posters will be seen by twenty thousand customers over five days
- *Motivators*: the specific payoff they need that will spur them to action—through the posters you'll be able to reach your key market of mothers with young children

When you have built up a list of motivators for a specific donor, focus on what the key ones are—what the hot buttons are.

Notes

1. See F. Herzberg, "One More Time: How Do You Motivate Employees?" *Harvard Business Review* (January-February 1968): 53–62.

Part Two

Proposal

4

MAKING YOUR CASE

In this chapter we look at how to shape your fundraising *Proposal*—often expressed as a case—to make sure it is organized for maximum impact on the prospect or donor. Although the focus is on written cases, the same principles apply to anyone preparing for a one-to-one meeting, drafting an e-mail, or shaping a PowerPoint presentation.

Specifically we explore

- A framework for cases to help clarify what your basic proposition is from the four key options available
- Ideas and techniques on how to create powerful proposals when you can't meet your prospect face-to-face and you need to write ideas down
- The five key questions that a case needs to answer to enable stakeholders—both internal and external—to engage with it
- The four key principles to apply to "good" language that will make it easy to read *and* easy to write
- The importance of metaphors and other imaginative approaches when you want to capture the essence of your proposal in a memorable way

Writing for Fundraising Influence

The act of writing for influence is not necessarily natural or easy, but it's an essential skill in fundraising—especially in a world of e-mails and PowerPoint presentations. Writing can help you improve your case in a number of ways. These include

- *Clarifying* your own thinking about a topic or an issue
- *Distilling* the thoughts of a group of trustees or volunteers

- *Answering* a challenge that's been raised
- *Defining* expectations in a letter of agreement

Written fundraising communication can also take a number of forms, each of which asks for different responses. For example:

- A 146-character text message sent by SMS (short message service) to supporters' mobile phones calling for instant action
- A Web-page encouraging a potentially interested party to click on a link and find out more about a cause
- A leaflet or brochure picked up at an event that the prospect takes home to read in his or her own time

All of these formats are opportunities for influence. Many of them will draw on a central structure commonly referred to as a case statement.

What Is a Case Statement?

A case statement or case for support is the core document sitting at the center of your fundraising strategy. It explains to potential supporters what you need money for and what the benefits will be to the beneficiaries if they donate to your cause. A case is normally written by a campaign team or sometimes by a specialist writer. Either way it's a program of action designed to influence and engage internal and external stakeholders in your work or campaign.

Cases can be used in a range of fundraising settings, but they are viewed as essential in major gift, capital, and endowment campaigns.

A case is powerful and effective if it is

- A clear, widely owned and understood vision of what is to be achieved

- A defined and costed list of the resources needed to achieve that vision
- Aimed at a cluster of donors who have the potential to meet the expressed need

Once written, the case is often used as the source for other communications, such as brochures, proposals, presentations, and even speeches at events. It therefore forms an important part of your influence toolkit.

Who Is a Case Statement For?

For your case to be successful it needs to appeal to a number of different stakeholders. (We're using *stakeholder* to describe the range of parties and individuals involved with and interested in your organization.)

Cases are often thought of as just for *external* stakeholders—donors, in particular. But they need to address *internal* stakeholders too. The person who answers the switchboard might not appear to be very important in the great scheme of things. But the way he or she responds to donors calling in could make a massive difference to your success. So the case should influence internal stakeholders—including that vital person who answers the phone—on how to respond to donor queries and challenges.

Different stakeholder groupings have different needs and concerns. Sometimes these needs and concerns are not directly about the cause itself, but about how they can get involved, what you expect of them, and what they expect of you. For your case to have influence you need to ensure it answers these questions.

In Table 4.1 we give some examples of typical stakeholder groupings and their concerns.

You might like to review your current case document if you have one and consider how many of these stakeholders it is designed for and how many of these questions it answers.

Table 4.1 Stakeholder Concerns

Stakeholder	Needs and Concerns Questions
Board members	Will this case be deliverable? How do we specifically help, apart from cash? What will our contribution be?
Volunteers	Will our role be preserved or extended? How do we work alongside staff in this? What will our contribution be?
Staff	Are there any risks to our jobs or roles? What new skills and roles will this ask of us? Will this distract from "normal" work?
Senior managers	What new competencies do we need? Do we have the staff to carry this out? Will the board or CEO provide us with support?
Funders or donors	Will this idea succeed if I fund it? What will the scale of my commitment be? Who else is involved or committed?
Regulators[1]	Are there any potential pitfalls in this? Will this create a precedent to consider? What rules and regulations are involved?
Beneficiaries	Will this commitment be delivered? How will we directly benefit? Is this really meeting our needs?

Challenges with Cases

In our experience there are three key problems in the way many cases are currently written by fundraisers following the "classic" models:

- *They're too internally focused:* Many cases we've read are obsessed with the organization's structural concerns or use technical, hard-to-understand language that is inaccessible to anyone not on the staff. By not focusing enough on the needs of the beneficiaries or the concerns of the donors, they become self-referential or even indulgent.

- *They're too long:* The best case might exist in several forms—from fifty pages of detailed and costed development opportunities with specified outcomes to a one-page executive summary. But ideally the proposition should be able to stand alone as a simple one-liner, such as Oxfam's "Make Poverty History."

- *They're too fixed:* Major donors, in our experience, don't want to be given a *finished* plan to fund. They want to be involved in its *development.* So you need to create space for them to contribute, and be prepared to add in their ideas. This engagement can even form part of your influence strategy.

=mc Case Framework

The case statement should provide a solid basis on which to communicate your need. It needs to be more than just a snappy mission statement or punchy slogan. But it also needs to be less than a lengthy philosophical enquiry into why your organization should exist.

Despite what you may have learned elsewhere, believe us when we say it *will* have to end up existing in *several* forms—a longer version with detailed data and analysis backup, and a shorter, pithier one that encapsulates the central idea. For example, we wrote a thirty-page document for a disability charity in the United Kingdom covering five sophisticated "vision propositions" for people with the disability. The work took several months—we did interviews; we ran focus groups with staff, users, and other stakeholders; we ran an online survey. The result was a detailed, closely argued case backed by a robust budget. Then one day we had an urgent call from the appeal director. We met with her the same afternoon. Together we wrote a six-line version of the case for a key networker to use at a reception being hosted by the British prime minister at 6:30 that evening. It had to be just as compelling as the thirty-page version, because it was the equivalent of a movie studio elevator pitch designed to raise "big money."

A case can be translated not just into different forms but also into a whole *series of messages* to reach a variety of donors and supporters. But first you need to decide what the *fundamental* message is. At =mc we've developed a framework to help you do this, which we've used successfully with many of our customers—from a gallery raising $50 million to purchase a Renaissance painting, to an international child care charity raising $500 million across twenty-seven countries to provide education for children in conflict zones.

The framework assumes that all cases can be based on two dimensions:

- *Time:* whether the outcome will happen now, soon, or at some future point
- *Impact:* whether the case will work *toward* a positive or *away* from a negative

If you put these dimensions together in all the possible combinations, you have four choices:

A positive present: in other words, an *opportunity*. This

- Has a relatively short time horizon
- Is about a *positive* outcome

A negative present: in other words, a *crisis*. This

- Also has a relatively short time horizon
- Is about a *negative* outcome

A positive future: in other words, a *vision*. This

- Encourages the donor to think far ahead
- Is about a *positive* outcome

A negative future: in other words, a *risk*. This

- Also encourages the donor to think far ahead
- Is about a *negative* outcome

Better still, put them in a matrix:

	Present	Future
Positive	Opportunity	Vision
Negative	Crisis	Risk

Each of these choices is illustrated in the following examples for two different organizations—one an HIV/AIDS development agency in Africa and the other a theater in a small U.S. city.

HIV/AIDS Example

- *Opportunity:* "If we can organize the condom distribution program effectively in the next six months, we can reduce infection by 60 percent in Zimbabwe."
- *Vision:* "By building the new center and equipping it properly, we can ensure that within ten years every person in Zimbabwe will have access to anti-retrovirals."
- *Crisis:* "At current rates of infection and with the current limited access to anti-retrovirals, 100,000 people in Zimbabwe will die needlessly in the next six months."
- *Risk:* "Unless we use condoms and education programs to stem the growth of HIV transmission, in ten years there will be five million AIDS orphans in Zimbabwe."

Theater Example

- *Opportunity:* "Thanks to a shop closure, the building lease has come free on a large space next door.

If we raise the money in the next three months,
we can acquire the space for the experimental
studio we've been talking about for years."

- *Vision:* "If we raise the cash, we can extend into
the premises next door. With that extra ten thousand square feet, we'd gain experimental space to
complement our main platform *and* craft work-
shops. In five years we'll be the leading arts center in
the city."

- *Crisis:* "If we don't find funds for the roof repairs
within the next three months, we will have to close
the building. The loss of cash from the box office
will be so great we may never reopen. Our town
will have lost its only purpose-built theater."

- *Risk:* "If we don't secure the funds for the education program, then within five years there will be a
whole generation denied access to culture—up to
three thousand eighteen-year-olds in this town who
will have never seen a live theater performance."

You need to decide which of the quadrants your case falls
into most naturally. It might fit all of them in a *general* sense, but
what you need for a case is *focus.*

It's interesting to us which of these is the most powerful
quadrant in fundraising. Take a second to reflect on which you
believe normally works best.

We've asked that question in over twenty conference sessions
in places as far apart as Brazil, India, Australia, and Sweden.
Almost universally, *experienced* fundraisers know the answer.
Most of them wish it could be "vision" (positive future). In
practice—from their experience—they know "crisis" (negative
present) is normally the strongest. The psychology of this is
complex but can, in part, be traced back to Maslow, whose
hierarchy of needs is based on *unmet* needs. It's worth your while
to always have an option to frame your case as a crisis. (And it's

useful, if you can, to have your case expressed in all four forms to allow for maximum flexibility.)

Five Key Questions to Drive the Structure of a Case

Whatever quadrant your case statement sits in, it needs to answer some key questions—questions that also help you create a useful structure.

- *What is the need?* Your answers to this question should explain what *exactly* the need is and who *exactly* will benefit when that need is met. You should be able to scale the need so that donors or supporters can understand where they can make a *difference* even if they can't solve the whole challenge. ("World poverty" is too big for anyone to fix. Saving a child or a family, or a village, or even—if you're Bill Gates—a country, is more manageable.)

- *What evidence is there that this is a pressing need?* It's not really worth pointing out a need unless you can demonstrate that it must be tackled *soon*. Otherwise you may lose ground to other causes. Your evidence could include surveys, expert opinions, or beneficiary statements. (World poverty's been around a long time—why the rush to fix it now?)

- *How is your organization uniquely qualified to tackle this need?* It's likely there are a number of agencies qualified to tackle this issue. What's special about you—your track record, the novelty of your approach, what? How will you build confidence and credibility? (What bits of world poverty can you alone tackle?)

- *What will be the benefits of your action?* What positive consequences will there be if you take action on this need? What will be major benefits and what will be minor consequences? What can you *guarantee* and what is *possible* but not definite? (In what way will we notice world poverty reducing?)

- *What are the negative consequences if you fail?* Sometimes the key drivers for the donor are negative. (This fits with our crisis-as-priority perception.) People would like to stop something awful happening or continuing. You should be able to explain the major and minor negative consequences. (How many more of the world's children will grow up in poverty if you don't succeed?)

When you're developing your case, use these questions to guide your collection of data. We think you'll find them helpful. Of course, you then need to answer the hardest question—why should the donor or other stakeholder care? The rest of this book helps you tackle that issue.

Good Written Communication

It's slightly embarrassing to have to include a section on "good" writing in a book about influence. But the simple reality is we often find that charities write in a formal and slightly anemic academic way or a florid and over-emotional way about their causes. Neither of these is good writing.

Here we share some basic principles that will ensure your writing is clearer and more powerful. This is not an exercise in aesthetics, but is simply included because clearer writing is more likely to achieve influence.

Our experience of reading and writing fundraising proposals—and more important, our experience of asking donors about their reaction to different cases—suggests there are four fundamental rules of any good written communication. By following these you can increase the chances of successful influence on the page.

These rules are

1. Favor shorter, familiar words
2. Keep most sentences short
3. Use active verbs
4. Put people in your writing

1. Favor Shorter, Familiar Words

Shorter words are, in general, easier to use and to understand. For example, use *help* not *facilitate* and *cash bequest* rather than *pecuniary bequest*. Your communication will be read more quickly and will be more widely understood.

We're not saying that you should never use long words— sometimes they're necessary. So in a specific situation you may need to use a technical word such as *endowment* or *governance*. But do not use longer or more complicated words than you have to. Why use *facilitate* when *help* means the same and is easier to understand? People tend to use longer words to try to impress or to cover up weak thinking. Don't fall into that trap.

In the following list we've taken some words we've found in various case statements and suggested simpler replacements.

Complex Word	Simpler Word
utilize	use
sufficient	enough
ongoing	continuous
endeavor	try
remuneration	pay
in the event that	if

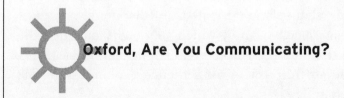

Oxford, Are You Communicating?

As part of the research for this book we randomly typed "legacies" into Google. ("Legacies" is the U.K. word for bequest.) At the top of the list was a prestigious and respected college in Oxford University. Our first reaction was to be impressed. Coming at the top of the Google list is great—especially if you're looking for money. And if we had been random millionaires looking to make a bequest, we'd have begun by considering the college. But then we looked at how the college shared its case. And the more we read the less impressed we were.

Yes, they have a first-hit Website that explains why they need money, but the language they use is the worst kind of prose. For example, one of the major benefits of making a gift to the college is that "Well-wishers are enumerated in the list of benefactors...." We *think* that means, "People who have made a gift have their names read out...." Who are they trying to impress here? Would you like to be "enumerated"? Aren't well-wishers people who come around to your house at Christmas and bring tidings of comfort and joy?

It gets worse. Here's a sample from the "easy-to-understand" Q and A section they've included on the site.

"Q: Whom should I talk with about this?

A: It is of paramount importance to speak with your own financial and legal advisors when making such decisions [about making a bequest or major gift]. Also, the information contained here is provided as a suggestion of possible means by which you may provide for the college in your estate planning. It is therefore axiomatic that you speak with qualified estate planning experts to determine the most appropriate mechanism by which you might maximize the tax and charitable benefits deriving from your bequest."

That last thirty-two-word sentence is a killer. We *think* they were trying to say this:

"It's essential that you consult a qualified estate planning expert—such as a lawyer or accountant—before making a bequest or any other gift to the college. This expert can help you find the most effective way for you *and* the college to receive the maximum benefit from your generous gift."

Sorry to be blunt, Oxford college, but you need to write much more simply and clearly if you really want to communicate and influence.

Go through your own written documents and get rid of complex language.

2. Keep Most Sentences Short

By short sentences we mean ideally seventeen words or less. Shorter sentences are easier to read *and* easier to write. Note that short and simple don't mean *simplistic*. Highbrow newspapers such as the *Times* in the United Kingdom and the *Wall Street Journal* in the United States both use a stylebook that asks journalists to write in short sentences. The logic here is straightforward. Busy people don't have the time to spend the whole day reading the newspaper. Nor do donors. Short sentences speed up reading.[2]

Another failing of long sentences is that they may hide key messages from donors by combining too many of them. Here's an example:

"The Southtown Advice Center has a pressing need for funds to upgrade its IT-based reference systems to help staffers to be more effective and so provide better quality information on welfare benefits for socially excluded people in the local area."

By making a long sentence you minimize the advantage to be gained from the IT upgrade. Contrast this with:

"The Southtown Advice Center urgently needs to upgrade its computer systems. If we can raise the money for the upgrade, staff will be able to provide better information on benefits for poor people in the area."

(Notice we've lost the long and unnecessary words too.)

3. Use Active Verbs

The use of passive verbs in fundraising writing also holds us back from communicating and influencing effectively. The difference between active and passive is simple. Contrast "The boy bounced the ball" (active) with "The ball was bounced by the boy" (passive). The passive is clumsy, and can also hide responsibility for the action.

Another example. Compare "It has been identified that the Southtown Advice Center needs a new computer system" with "The Trustees commissioned a feasibility study from experienced independent consultants. Their recommendation is that we install a new computer system." It's clear in the second one who did what.

We've seen many board minutes that say something along the lines of "It was agreed that money should be raised for the new project." Usually such a minute is a death knell for the scheme. "*Who* will do *what?*" is a key question in fundraising. And *active* sentences always answer that question.

4. Put People in Your Writing

There's a misguided view that good writing is impersonal. It's sometimes called using the *third person*. But this approach can make your case sound "cold" or—again—pseudo-academic. When you put yourself and the people you want to help in your case statement you gain two benefits. First, your writing is more alive and engaging. And second, you're forced to think about whom you're writing *for*.

Let's go back to the advice center. "Help with benefits is available at the advice center" is not going to encourage local people to come in. Much better to say, "If you need help with benefits, then there is a team of five trained staff at the center who can help." Or, compare "Funds can ensure the long-term future of the arts center's education outreach program" with "We need committed donors keen to make a significant investment to help our trained educators continue their work with young people in schools."

The Ten Commandments as an Influence Communication

Whether they're Christian or not, most people accept that the Ten Commandments are a powerful—and influential—piece of communication. But how do the commandments achieve this power? Not through complex grammar or by using long words. Take, for example, "Thou shalt not steal." That's a pretty clear and straightforward injunction. You know that if you do steal, God will be pretty cheesed off.

Think about your own organization's policy on expenses. You probably have pages of text on the subject, including several lines on acceptable forms of tax receipts. Can you apply the discipline of the Ten Commandments to your communication?

Metaphors

One of the most powerful and neglected aspects of influence in general, and cases in particular, is the power of metaphors. A metaphor—from the Greek source, "to carry meaning"—is a figure of speech in which one thing or idea is linked to another.

Metaphors are popular and common in literature, especially among great writers. Have a look at any work by Dickens, Dante, or Whitman. The very best metaphors engage us in a powerful, emotional way. Read, for example, the opening of Dickens's *Bleak House*, with its description of fog as a metaphor for moral uncertainty. But metaphors are not just the preserve of "high" culture. For many people, Forrest Gump's "Life is like a box of chocolates" is a powerful metaphor (though it's really a simile) for accepting all parts of life—the bits you don't enjoy along with those you do. Hokey, but it works for some.

Technically, metaphors are different from a range of other written techniques, such as similes, analogies, and parables. But for the purposes of this chapter, let's assume they all serve as a means to emotionally engage those we wish to influence.

In what's come to be known as his "I have a dream" speech, Martin Luther King Jr. proves himself a master of metaphor. He talks about "Negro slaves who had been seared in the flames of withering injustice," "the quick sands of racial injustice," and "the solid rock of justice." He has a dream that Mississippi, "a state sweltering with the heat of injustice, sweltering with the heat of oppression, will be transformed into an oasis of freedom and justice." The richness and variety of the language and the images he conjures carry King's audience along on an unstoppable wave of anger and optimism even today, more than forty years later.

One notable contemporary example of a widely used influence metaphor, which has been hugely useful for the environmental movement, is Gaia. The name *Gaia*—symbolizing the ancient Greek goddess of the earth—was taken by James Lovelock to make concrete the idea of the planet as a living organism, with which people have to cohabit in harmony. Among others, Greenpeace and Friends of the Earth have used Gaia to explain to donors why environmental concern is not just about recycling. It's about a way of life that allows us to share the living organism that is the earth's space.

Here are some examples of successful metaphors we've helped develop for influencers:

- The CEO of a major U.K. cultural agency wanted to undertake a fundamental and unpopular restructure that would involve a number of independent regional agencies being merged into one centralized body after twenty-five years of autonomy. On the day he wrote to all of the regional directors outlining his ideas, he began his letter with a metaphor, "The train is leaving the station." He used the same metaphor several times in his communications throughout the difficult process that lay ahead. His intention was to signal that the merger was something that was *going* to happen and *would* happen on a *specific date*. And the regional directors had to "get on board the train" or "be left behind at the station." People got the message. And despite resistance, eventually most of them got on the train.

- We worked with a group of senior Brazilian educators and community activists who wanted to seek support from senior businesspeople for their NGO, Comunitas. They wanted to position their approach as one that wasn't simply about philanthropy but also about making sure young Brazilians grew up confident and capable. We developed the metaphor of a "social IPO." The case statement used the language of a stock market listing, designed to appeal to business people. We incorporated phrases such as "the triple bottom line," "return on *social* investment," and "*creative* cash flow." Investors loved the metaphor and the appeal raised $10 million in four weeks.

- You may not have noticed, but in June 2007 the person elected to be CEO of Caritas International, the charitable wing of the Catholic Church, was a woman, Lesley Anne Knight. She is the first woman to secure the post in the organization's four-hundred-year history. We coached Lesley Anne in her pitch to the three hundred delegates who had gathered in Rome for the election. Lesley Anne wanted to make it clear she was keen to involve liberal *and* more conservative elements of the church.

She used a number of biblical metaphors, including "my father's house has many rooms," to signal her openness to different points of view. She won the support of the delegates and was duly elected CEO.

More Than Just Words

Sometimes words are not enough. To get around this, we've often used a technique in which "physical things"—objects, tools, and so on—are used as metaphors.

We are lucky to have been involved in some fabulous examples of "things" as fundraising metaphors. For instance, we worked with the prestigious British Film Institute on its fundraising case. Much of its work is about preserving historically interesting films from the 1920s, 1930s, and 1940s. And much of that work is quite prosaic, transferring movies from old, unstable nitrate-based stock to new digital media. It's vital work if you want to preserve the cultural heritage, but hard to make engaging. Working with the director of development, we came up with an idea.

When she met a donor, the director first presented her case for protecting the cinematic heritage. Next she would ask what the donor's favorite old movie was. She would then produce a strip of film from a labeled tin and rub it between her fingers, allowing it to crumble into a pile of ash-like material on the desk or table. She'd pause and then say, "That's what's happening to the original of your favorite film right now. And to many other vital films." The donor would look aghast and, with their eyes never leaving the distressing ash pile, usually commit.

If you can come up with a "physical" metaphor and use it to turn on the senses in a powerful way your case will be much stronger. (See Chapter Eight, "Speaking the Language of Influence," for more on this.) You can even do this in a group. A Mexican domestic violence charity we worked with held a dinner for donors on an empty piece of land. The meal, an open-air barbecue done in the family style, symbolized that the donors were the "family" who were to build this house for women who had violent partners.

Brick as Fundraising Metaphor

In Bolivia there's a priest, Fr. Luis, who uses a brick as his vision and fundraising case. We met him at a Council on Foundations meeting in Chicago. When we first saw him he was in the lobby of the convention hotel sitting at a table and waving the brick at the president of a very important foundation who sat opposite. To see a priest waving a brick at a conference is, you might think, strange. What was stranger was that the president of this foundation didn't look anxious at all. In fact she was smiling. And as we watched dumbstruck we saw her get up, smile even more broadly, and then shake hands with the priest.

Slightly nervous, we approached him and asked what he had been doing with the brick. He offered to explain. Fr. Luis had come to Bolivia as a young man from Spain, and had begun his pastoral work helping poor people in remote villages. One day when he'd stopped in a village, a ten-year-old boy had come to him clutching something and asked, "Father, is this any use as a brick?" The priest looked down and saw what the boy had in his hands. Although of a similar size and shape as a brick, it was in fact a thick book—an encyclopedia. He explained to the child that his "brick" was no good as a brick, but it was a very useful book. The boy was bitterly disappointed, and threw away the book. "Well it's useless if it's not a brick—I'm helping build a house. And anyway I can't read."

The priest was shocked. But he realized he couldn't convince the child of the book's value if the boy couldn't read. So in the great tradition of radical Latin American priests, he there and then decided to focus his work on literacy. Now a man on a very concrete mission, he set up the rather grandly titled Bolivian Traveling Peasant Library. (In reality the "library" was a donkey with some books on its back.) As he worked to raise funds for the project, the priest found himself repeating to donors the story of what had moved him to start it. And he found that the "metaphor" of the boy who thought bricks were more useful than a book had huge impact. So he began to carry a brick everywhere he went to illustrate his campaign.

Which is why he had the brick at the meeting we had witnessed. He'd produced it to say to the funder, "Your money can help young people learn that books are more important than bricks!" She had smiled because she identified with his sentiment.

Fr. Luis was nothing if not pragmatic. Once he'd told us about the brick, he showed us his formal written proposal. It was full of data detailing the scale of the literacy issue. For example, Chusisaca, where he works, is one of the poorest areas in Bolivia. Average income is only $240 a year, and the literacy rate is 21.3 percent—lower, even, than in Haiti. It was a powerful set of facts and a powerful case for change. "But," he said to us smiling broadly, "it's not the proposal, it's the brick that moves people. The proposal is great for after. But donors really get it when I show them the brick."

We now use the idea of a brick as a metaphor in our own work with influencers and especially fundraisers. We ask them, "What's the brick?" meaning what is your *one defining example* of the challenge—or the solution—that you have?

A good *brick*—like a good metaphor—has three key characteristics. It is

- *Simple*—You can say it in sixty seconds or less.
- *Memorable*—When they've read it (or heard it) people can repeat it later.
- *Powerful*—It creates a strong emotional response.

Summary

In fundraising you often need to express your passion as a *written
proposal* that others can engage with. This proposal becomes a
way to influence internal and external stakeholders.

The most common format—although not the only one for a
proposal—is called a case statement. There are numerous books
on how to write a case statement. The implication of this chapter,
and indeed of this book, is that many of them are flawed and fail
to take account of donors' psychological and communications
preferences.

To be of use to donors, a good case needs to answer five key
questions:

- What is the need?
- What evidence is there that this is a pressing need?
- How is your organization uniquely qualified to tackle this need?
- What will be the benefits of your action?
- What are the negative consequences if you fail?

Any communication that answers these questions will be
powerful. You need to answer just one more question to make it
perfect:

- Why should the donor care?

A case is one of the most usual formats for a proposal. At =mc we have developed a model with four main case options. All of these involve *time* and *outcome*. The four options are vision, opportunity, risk, and crisis. You *should* be able to frame your influence proposition in all four—but remember that *crisis* is the strongest.

If you are going to write as part of your influence initiative, follow four simple rules:

1. Favor shorter, familiar words

2. Keep most sentences short

3. Use active verbs

4. Put people in your writing

Increasingly, organizations and high-level influencers are working on creative ways to express proposal and other fundraising ideas. One powerful way to do this is through metaphors. Metaphors can be written but they can also use other senses such as touch or smell. If you use metaphors—or another member of the same linguistic family such as analogy or simile—you'll find these are useful ways to give your case some extra punch.

Notes

1. Often there are regulators involved—city officials, federal legislators, trustees, and so on. Which ones depends on your proposition.
2. The reason many of us write in long sentences—average thirty-five words—is because it's the "academic style" encouraged by colleges and universities that many fundraisers attend.

Part Three

Preparation

5

SHAPING OUTCOMES

A key element in your *Preparation* is a specific, measurable, and achievable—or well-formed—outcome. The methodology outlined in this chapter will ensure that you are able to identify what you want, and what the prospect or donor wants, in a fundraising influence situation.

Preparation should involve a certain amount of background research. But the *focus* needs to be on the prospect's potential and propensity to contribute to your outcome.

In this chapter we specifically help you

- Distinguish between an *outcome* and what is conventionally called a *fundraising goal*
- Explore how to ask *yourself* questions as you go through a seven-step process designed to help you frame your outcome
- Explore how to use the LIM-it technique to balance the desired outcome with flexibility about what's practical and possible

The result is you'll be able to go into any influence situation clear in your mind about the internal and external evidence that will spell success.

Tell *Yourself* What You Want

Preparation is the third "P" in our framework. Like successful fundraising itself, successful influence needs to be underpinned by solid, detailed thinking in advance—especially about what would be an acceptable result. We suggest you focus your preparation on working out what you *really want to achieve* with the prospect, and what *might be possible or acceptable*. If you're not certain about the outcome you're aiming for, how do you know if you've succeeded? Being certain about the outcome doesn't mean you only have one choice. But it does mean you can be certain about the *options* you could agree to.

Paralysis by Analysis

Unfortunately, many fundraisers trained in the "old-fashioned" school of moves management believe preparation means simply "finding out everything you possibly can about the prospect." So that's where they spend much of their time. Let's quickly consider the value of this time investment.

As we've said, our experience is that that kind of obsession with "biographical" preparation—where this person went to school, what their hobbies are, and so on—doesn't really have the payoff you might imagine it should.

Let's be clear. We're *not* saying don't bother researching background information on the prospect. A certain level of biographical information—especially on their *propensity* and *potential* to give—is undoubtedly helpful, and it *is* an important part of the preparation. Depending on the context of your prospect meeting, and the ability of your organization to provide research backup, you might well expect to find out

☐ Information on an individual's family and friends

☐ Their interests—such as hobbies and cultural interests

☐ Their education—to what level and where they were educated

☐ Any strong faith or political affiliation they have

☐ Any other causes they have supported in a significant way

☐ Some estimate of their wealth or likely ability to give

However, there are two problems with prospect research as your *only* preparation. First, the reality is you can't often get all that information, or some of it may be of dubious provenance. Second, some fundraisers move into a comfort zone of what seems like almost permanent preparation, believing they can't have a meeting with a donor until they have "perfect" data. So they never make that call or write that case. This is *paralysis by analysis*.

Shaping a Well-Formed Outcome

Prospect research is what we call passive preparation—you're only finding out what is the case or has been the case with that person. To *actively* prepare, your priority is to create what we call a *well-formed outcome*. This is a clear, rich, positive description of the result you want. It has more depth and is more useful for influence than a simple fundraising *goal*. (A fundraising goal generally merely defines the size of a gift, from whom it comes, and by when—"To secure a $500,000 gift from Ms. Smith at the meeting on June 5.")

A well-formed outcome, in contrast, allows you to respond to circumstances and adjust your behavior—and even the outcome—to ensure you arrive at the *best possible result*.

Let's distinguish between a *goal* and an *outcome*.

A goal . . .	An outcome . . .
Is about a fundraising result in terms of money	Is about a positive situation you want to arrive at
Provides evidence of success at the end of the process	Provides evidence as you go along as well as at the end
Is binary—can be judged only as a success or failure	Is flexible, allowing you to adjust to what's possible
Tracks the interests of the asker	Tracks the interests of both parties
Stresses one kind of data—the financial result	Emphasizes rich sensory data, including the financial result

To a fundraiser it may seem obvious what the outcome is—as much money as possible from the donor for the cause. But it's not always as simple as that. True, money is normally the *ultimate* outcome, but there can be others:

- To persuade an individual to provide you with a high-level introduction to someone else
- To reassure an anxious donor who is nervous or reluctant to engage with your cause
- To encourage a donor to make a "breakthrough" gift rather than an "ordinary" gift that fits with their past philanthropy
- To secure agreement from a donor to become a super ambassador on your behalf, not simply giving money but *championing* the cause

If you *don't* have a well-formed outcome there are negative consequences. You may

- Handle the situation badly and perhaps run the risk of souring the relationship permanently
- End up with a less effective result—much less money?—than you might have secured

And, ironically, worst of all you may

- Succeed, but you won't really know *how* or *why*—so you'll have to go through the whole learning curve again.

A well-formed outcome fits well with your needs, interests, and values, and *ideally* with those of the donor.

Outcome Before Means

An outcome is the *result* you want—the *what*. It's *not* something you *do*—the *how*.

If you start with the *how* without being clear about the *what*, you can end up failing simply because the task is inappropriate for the result. For example, you organize a private dinner for an individual donor when that person responds best in a group. Or you set up a peer ask when a personal appeal from a golfing hero would be a better motivator.

There's one other reason we're encouraging you to focus on outcome, not methodology. If you're specific about *what you want* at the outset, you can then concentrate on building flexibility into your *approach*. If one way doesn't work, fine—try another.

Seven Steps to Establishing the Outcome You Want

A successful outcome for your influence initiative is one that fits your needs and interests as well as the prospect's. To prepare for that result, we suggest seven steps:

Step 1: Be clear what you want.
Step 2: Establish the evidence.

> *Step 3:* Consider the context.
>
> *Step 4:* Establish what resources you control.
>
> *Step 5:* Consider the consequences.
>
> *Step 6:* Anticipate challenges.
>
> *Step 7:* Develop a flexible plan.

Step 1: Be Clear What You Want

Most of us tend to go into situations too vague about what exactly it is that we want—"To get a substantial gift" or "To engage Ms. Jones in the cause."

To clarify your outcome effectively make sure it's positive and *specific*.

Positive: An outcome described in positive terms is more powerful than one described in negative terms. Yet often we approach a meeting thinking, "I hope I don't say the wrong thing" or "I really don't want to appear nervous," with the result that we make the very mistake we're hoping to avoid.

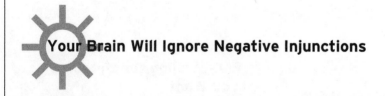

Your Brain Will Ignore Negative Injunctions

If we say to you "Don't think about bananas," what immediately pops into your head? It's not, by any chance, a picture of a curved fruit—yellow skin, soft interior? There's an important psychological principle at work here. Your brain is not very good at recognizing and responding to *negatives*, which means it often deletes words such as *don't*—leaving us with "(don't) think about bananas...." (This phenomenon also helps explain why people often have challenges with life goals such as "I must not eat French fries" or "I need to give up smoking." The negative element in the goals—*stop* and *give up*—are misted over by the brain, leaving "I must eat fries" and "I need to smoke.")

So instead of expressing your influence outcome as "Prevent this donor from leaving the board," try "Get the donor to recommit to a three-year term."

Specific: The outcome you describe must be sufficiently concrete both to keep you focused on it and for it to represent a *possible* achievement. (See the following section, "Know your LIM-its.") It should be neither too modest nor a fantasy. To help, you might imagine the person saying, "Well that's a gift way beyond what the foundation had considered. But after the way you've put the case I'm recommending 'yes' to the other trustees."

Specific doesn't mean unchangeable—you can adapt the outcome if it proves unrealistic. But specific beats vague every time. In 1954 the U.K. athlete Roger Bannister set himself the goal "to run a four-minute mile," not "to run as fast as I can." The specification of the four-minute mile gave Bannister a very clear focus against which all his improvements (and setbacks) could be measured on the road to success. The more concretely you can imagine your goal or outcome, the more achievable it will be.

Know Your LIM-its It's sometimes difficult to know whether a prospect's potential is, say, $250,000 or $2 million. So how do you avoid setting a specific goal that is *meaningless*? How do you make it challenging but *possible*? We use a technique called the LIM-it, adapted from an idea by consultant Gavin Kennedy. (His excellent book, *Everything Is Negotiable*, is listed in the bibliography.) The LIM-it is especially useful when you're negotiating a company sponsorship, but it can be applied to many fundraising situations.

LIM stands for *Like, Intend,* and *Must,* and the "-it" encourages you to think of maximums and minimums (limit). Specifically,

- *Like:* This is what you *ideally want*—a $5 million one-off gift, or a three-year sponsorship deal.
- *Intend:* This is what you *can accept*—a gift between $2 and $3 million, or a two-year sponsorship deal.
- *Must:* This is the *minimum you need* or can accept, and if you don't get it, it's no deal—a gift of $.5 million for the naming rights, or sponsorship for a project.

The LIM-it technique is useful in that it forces you to think in terms of a *range* of possible solutions, and in an influence situation that then allows you to be specific *and* flexible. There are a number of different ways to calculate your LIM-it. But the most important elements are

- To set what you'd *Like* to get high enough so that *your* needs are reflected in the best possible outcome.
- To frame what you *Intend* to get as something that you believe might meet the interests of *both* parties.
- To be confident in what you *Must* get so that if for any reason that outcome is not achievable you can walk away.

Understanding the LIM-its of the Corporate Mind

LifeRace is a fictional cancer charity seeking support for its Women's Cancer Run from the insurance agent Driverco (also fictional). Driverco only insures women drivers.

LifeRace's event is obviously socially worthwhile. So Driverco offers the charity a modest philanthropic-style CSR

(corporate social responsibility) investment. But Blanca, LifeRace's head of corporate affairs, came from the private sector herself. She's well aware that Driverco could potentially gain a significant commercial benefit from its association with the cause far in excess of what it's offering under CSR.

Blanca calculates LifeRace could provide a number of straight marketing opportunities for Driverco. These range from name exposure—branding on runners' t-shirts, banners near the start and finish lines, logo on posters, and so on—to allowing the company to provide a goodie bag to every woman taking part that includes information on its insurance services. For Blanca, these possibilities mean she should have a LIM-it of *commercial* payoffs.

She prepares her LIM-it:

	Like	*Intend*	*Must*
Cash investment	$100,000 up-front; 10% of the value of any policy sold to participants	$75,000 up-front; 5% of the value of any policy sold	$50,000 up-front; $10 for every policy sold
Marketing support	Driverco to pay for race signage and t-shirts	Driverco to pay for race signage	Driverco to pay for the t-shirts
In-kind support	Driverco to provide one hundred race stewards from staff volunteers	Driverco to pay for lunch for any volunteers	Driverco to e-mail staff about volunteering

Blanca goes into the meeting with Driverco with her Like, Intend, and Must thought through. She gets her *Like* in cash investment and marketing support, and her *Intend* for in-kind support. Driverco is happy it's getting a good investment, and Blanca is happy with the level of support.

There are two key advantages to the LIM-it approach:

- It keeps you on track about what you want and whether you're getting it—or whether you need to or should change or adapt it
- When you're skilled in using it, you can, as Blanca did, swap between the elements

The LIM-it framework is most powerful when you also use it to establish *the donor's* Like, Intend, and Must. If we take the Life-Race example, Blanca would need to think through Driverco's LIM-it. Would Driverco *Like* sole branding or awareness opportunities and be prepared to pay more for that? Is the goodie bag with their information the most important element for them or simply an element they *Intend* to secure? Are the volunteering opportunities a *Must* because they are part of their retention strategy—or simply a *Like* element they want to add on? It's not always easy to work out someone else's LIM-it, but it's worth having a go as a way of shaping your preparation.

LIM-its are clearly very useful in a negotiation-type influence situation, and you can also use them to great effect with individual donors in a more philanthropic context. We'll come back to this in "Step 3: Consider the Context."

Step 2: Establish the Evidence

In creating a positive, concrete outcome you begin the process of preparing yourself for success. (You can think of it as loading up another useful piece of mental software.) To complete the process you need to think about the *modality* and the *metrics*. The *modality* is about *how* you will experience success in terms of seeing, hearing, and feeling. (For more on this, see Chapter Eight, "Speaking the Language of Influence.") The *metrics* are the specific *measures* or indicators of success.

Modality simply refers to how you will collect information on the outcome. There are three different sensory systems that you need to integrate to create a concrete outcome:

- *Vision*—What will you see? A smiling donor walking toward you? An outstretched hand? A thoughtful expression as she or he makes a difficult decision in your favor?
- *Sound*—What will you hear? The donor saying "Yes" in an exited tone? A softly spoken offer to consider the proposition? Clapping as others applaud your success?
- *Feeling*—What will you feel? Excited at the shake of the donor's hand? Relieved as you sit back in a soft chair in the donor's home? Pleasure as you reflect on the benefits the money will bring?

Imagining what success will be like *as exactly as possible* is a powerful technique to orient your actions and behavior. Note, you also need to be concerned about what *the donor or influence subject* will see, feel, and hear. In this way you can help them achieve *their* outcome insofar as it complements yours.

This is a version of a very powerful technique used by lots of athletes. Like many fundraisers, they only get one chance to get it right. Try watching the start of an Olympic 100-meter sprint and see the athletes mentally rehearsing not just the race, but the win.

One good example of an athlete doing this instinctively is Muhammad Ali. He used to mentally rehearse all his fights—and the outcomes—before the event. To do this he would change into his boxing gear and literally act out the fight in his bedroom, imagining how it would go almost blow-by-blow. At the moment of his imagined victory, he would then carefully "anchor"—or embed in his consciousness—the result he wanted. (See Chapter Six, "Building Self-Confidence.") At that moment he *saw* the flash of the reporters' bulbs recording his success, he *heard* the crowd chanting his name, and he recorded how he *felt*—and even smelled his own sweat as the referee lifted his right arm in a victory salute. Ali went into the ring psyched up to win and with the exact *metrics* and *modality* programmed into his brain.

So what can we learn from Muhammad Ali? How can fundraisers establish their own modality and what we call mental metrics for success? Table 5.1 gives some suggestions to help you get started.

Notice that the examples are discussed in the *present*—not what *will* happen but what *is* happening, as though that moment

Table 5.1 Modality and Mental Metric Suggestions

Modality	Mental Metrics
What does success *look* like? (Think about Muhammad Ali—he imagined the flash of the photographers' bulbs as they captured him succeeding.)	What do you see when you succeed—a smile, a check, a handshake? Who's there in your success picture—you, other donors, and beneficiaries? What are the details of the setting where this takes place—is it the donor's house, your office, at a project?
What does success *sound* like? (Ali heard the sound of the crowd chanting his name as a tribute to his victory, "Ali, Ali, Ali, Ali.")	What do you hear when you succeed? What is said? Who says it? What do you say? What kind of tone is agreement reached in—upbeat and excited or more reflective and considered? Do the words come fast or slow?
What does success *feel* like, and what are the *physical sensations*? (Ali smelled his sweat when he had mentally "won." Smell is a powerful aid to changing your emotional state. Ali also felt emotion as he acknowledged the crowd.)	What feelings do you have? Happy, proud, excited, relieved? What feeling does the donor have—anxious but excited, passionate, in touch with their values? If there's a handshake between you, is it firm and slow or fast and excited?

of success were *now*. Muhammad Ali didn't say "I *could* be the greatest," he said "I *am* the greatest."

The key task is to collect and program evidence into your brain on what success is like, so you'll *know when you've succeeded*. There are two kinds of useful evidence:

- *End result evidence:* that is, what *ultimate* success will look like, the final result you want—the verbal commitment to the gift, the writing of the check, the feeling of coming on board
- *Milestone evidence:* that is, what success will be like en route—for example, when a colleague offers to introduce you and you plan the introduction, when you get off the phone having successfully made the appointment to meet the donor

With an ambitious or long-term outcome, milestone evidence becomes particularly important both to keep you on track and to give you positive encouragement. In any event the mental metrics become the way you orient your behavior for influence results.

Step 3: Consider the Context

The *context* can make a significant difference to the outcome. Think about *where, when,* and *with whom* you will achieve the outcome. When you're doing this it's important you take into account the donor's point of view as well as your own.

Taking each element:

- *Where?* Where should this outcome happen? Where would be a good place for *you* and where not? And for the *donor?* And for the donor? What can you do to create that ideal setting?

- *When?* Is this an outcome for the next few weeks, the next few months, or for years ahead? Do you have a deadline you have to meet? What would be a good timeframe from your point of view? What timeframe is the donor working with?
- *With whom?* Who else should be there to help make the outcome possible? Who would be ideal from your point of view? Who would be ideal from the donor's point of view? (This also connects to the *resources* question in step 4.)

When considering the donor's needs and interests, think specifically about two things:

- Their *hygiene* factors and *motivations*. (See Chapter Three, "Understanding Donor Motivations.") So what reassurances (hygiene factors) might you have to give them before they will consider making the gift?
- What is their LIM-it? (See step 1.) You may not know exactly what their range of possible outcomes—Like, Intend, and Must—is. But it's useful to consider what it *might* be as a way of accessing their perceptions and concerns.

Step 4: Establish What Resources You Control

You will either have resources available—people or things—or you'll need to find some. Make a list of the *current* resources you have access to. When doing this, consider the following:

- *People:* Who can help? Colleagues, friends, other donors, senior volunteers? Are there role models you can turn to for advice, ideas, or even inspiration?
- *Settings:* Can you arrange the setting to make it work better? Can you change the ambience? What would be best—a formal or informal layout?

Next, still using "people" and "settings" as your triggers, make a second list of what *additional* resources would make your outcome more achievable. Be clear about what's genuinely important and what would be nice but isn't essential. Will a full-color brochure about your cause really swing the ask, or is the donor someone who won't necessarily respond well to a sophisticated PowerPoint presentation? Would a model of the proposed center help?

Finally, be clear about what resources you *don't have access to* and therefore cannot control. For example, if you can't produce a beautiful, slick, TV-quality DVD of the carnival project, what resources *do* you have that would help create the sense of wonder you believe the project engenders? A series of photographs? Testimonies or quotes from users?

The 360° Window Ask

At the University of Monterrey (UDEM) in Mexico, the two individuals in charge of development, Beto Viesca and Isabella Navarro, brilliantly exploited the resources they had to maximize the impact of their ask for a major capital campaign.

When the university was engaged in its first capital campaign it was still in the process of being built. Much of the campus was little more than a building site.

Undeterred, Beto and Isabella thought about how they could use this situation to their advantage. They decided to make their major donor asks in the main boardroom of the university. It had a huge panoramic window overlooking the emerging campus. Beto, the development director, would bring donors to this window and show them the gaps between completed buildings. Specifically, he identified the space where the building to which the donor was going to contribute was to stand. He encouraged the donor to mentally fill in the gap with the architect's plans that he or she had been shown, or the model that had been brought in. Often donors would defocus as they imagined "their" buildings filling specific gaps. It was a superb way to create a concrete and very real outcome for the donors.

Step 5: Consider the Consequences

There are usually wider issues arising from any outcome that you want. We call this the *ecology of the outcome you desire*. By ecology we mean two things:

- The extent to which the outcome fits with your organization's and the donor's values. No one should feel disappointed or uncomfortable.

- The likelihood of any outcome encouraging a long-term relationship. A gift achieved at the expense of the donor feeling manipulated is likely to scupper future partnerships.

For instance, you secure a grant from an alcohol company that helps your income target but alienates other key donors or sponsors who disagree with the ethics of taking money from such a company. A short-term win results in a long-term loss.

When considering the ecology of an outcome, it's useful to ask two key questions:

- What are the short- and long-term *advantages* of committing to this outcome—for me, for my organization, and for others?

- What are the potential *disadvantages* of committing to this outcome—for me, for my organization, and for others?

Even when you're sure you're behaving ethically there can be conflicts with values, either for you personally or for your organization.

- *Personal uncertainty:* In this case *you* may feel uncomfortable. For example, is this older person vulnerable when you speak to them about their gift? By reading this book you have access to a range of psychological techniques. Are you using them to help communicate your message better, or manipulatively? Another person may have the means and inclination to help your cause, but you may dislike their sexist attitude. How much sexism are you prepared to put up with? (And are they really sexist? Or is it that they're from an older generation or a different culture, and talking the way they do is considered acceptable?)

- *Organizational uncertainty:* Some organizational values might also have an impact on the way you go about raising money. For example, two leading U.K. charities disagree fundamentally on the propriety of a technique to secure bequest pledges. One is happy to organize events in elder care homes where residents approach their peers and ask if they would consider pledging a bequest. Another equally prestigious charity refuses to use this technique, believing it to be unethical. Who's right?

Step 6: Anticipate Challenges

There's a universal truth, "anything that can go wrong will go wrong." So you need to prepare for all the things that could stop you from achieving your well-formed outcome.

Following are some examples of the type of things you can expect to go wrong as you tread a path toward your result. All have a basis in harsh personal experience!

- How will you cope if you or the donor is late, and instead of having forty-five minutes for the "pitch" or meeting you have just twenty?
- What will you do if your computer or other technology doesn't work, and your beautiful presentation isn't available?
- How will you recover if you make some social gaffe? For example, if you forget someone's name, or provide a buffet with food that someone doesn't like?
- What will you do if the answer is "No" to your proposition? (We have a whole section on "Nine No's" in Chapter Ten, "Helping Donors Say 'Yes.'")

Step 7: Develop a Flexible Plan

Finally, you need to ensure that your plan with the donor is *flexible*. This relates mostly to dealing with the "challenges" issue in step 6.

We also suggest in step 1 that you should be flexible about your *outcome*. It sounds like an odd thing to recommend until you take into account the fact that sometimes you can make a judgment about what's possible based on too little or incorrect data. If that's the case, you need to be prepared to scale your ambition up or down once you possess updated information.

Chair-Based Wisdom

"If you ask for the gift and they fall off their chair, you've asked for too much. If you ask for the gift and they don't fall off their chair, you didn't ask for enough."

Of course the reality is that not many people actually fall off their chairs. But donors will give out subtle signals that will cue you as to whether your proposition is acceptable or not. In the meantime be clear about what is or isn't an acceptable outcome for *you*. Again, the LIM-it technique is helpful in this.

Summary

Having a well-formed outcome is an essential part of successful influence. It's more than a conventional fundraising goal, and should be at the center of your preparation.

A well-formed outcome has three characteristics. It is

- Positive
- Specific
- Based on sensory evidence

To arrive at that *outcome*, you need to follow a straightforward and methodical seven-step model.

Step 1: Be clear what you want—set your LIM-it: Like, Intend, Must. Try to establish what the donor wants, too.

Step 2: Establish the evidence—load up some mental software to describe what success will be like using the *modality* and *metrics* approach.

Step 3: Consider the context—where, when, and with whom will the outcome be achieved?

Step 4: Establish resources you control—understand what's under your control and what is not.

Step 5: Consider the consequences—think beyond your current outcome—if you achieved what you wanted are there any wider implications?

Step 6: Anticipate challenges—plan your response to things going wrong and how you might respond by changing tactics or your outcome.

Step 7: Develop a flexible plan—be prepared to adapt to changing circumstances. And be clear on what would be acceptable and unacceptable changes.

A vital tool for you in influence is the LIM-it. This encourages you to work out an acceptable range of outcomes:

- *Like*: what you ideally want
- *Intend*: what would be acceptable if not ideal
- *Must*: what you could live with but no less

A very skillful influencer will also try and work out the LIM-it for the other person or people involved. By giving them some of what *they* want you can often achieve what *you* want.

Finally, to be clear on what success will be like you need to describe your outcome in terms of

- *Modality*: What will you see, feel, and hear?
- *Metrics*: What exactly will happen, what objective data will there be of the outcome?

6

BUILDING SELF-CONFIDENCE—THE INNER GAME OF INFLUENCE

Much of this book is about communicating effectively with *others*. In this chapter we consider the need to "communicate" more effectively with *ourselves*. This is especially important in challenging influence situations in which the key to success is getting yourself into the most appropriate mind-set.

The approach we use is based on the principle of how you can "program" yourself with better mental software to make yourself more effective.

Specifically, we look at

- How you can build on previous occasions when you felt confident and competent about your influence
- How you can learn from other people who *are* successful and identify and copy the techniques and approaches they use
- How you can surround yourself with a cluster of *virtual advisers* to help you decide what to do in a challenging situation
- How you can sustain your self-confidence and that of colleagues in difficult situations

Confidence Is Key

Elsewhere in the book we discuss the importance of *appearing* confident and self-assured—and give you the techniques to do this. For a refresher on this, reread Chapter Five on setting goals and Appendix D, "Influencing in a Group." However, it can be much more challenging to ignore the negative audio track running in your head telling you that you're going to fail, that you're hopeless at this (whatever "this" is), and that people are going to see you can't do your job properly. And the mental track plays that much louder when

- You're a fundamentally shy and nervous person and feeling secure in yourself is alien territory.
- You've recently "blown" a major ask so your confidence is at an all-time low—and now you have to go and make another high-risk solicitation.
- A poor night's sleep with a crying baby has left you with a brain like mush and self-esteem that's flown out the window.

We're sure you've got your own examples. In any event, in these circumstances you need *practical* techniques to help you switch off the negative tape and develop the positive *inner feeling* that will complement your effective *outer behavior*.

In this chapter we share the three techniques that we've found hugely useful and that have helped to rescue fundraisers in critical influence situations:

- *Anchoring*: giving yourself access to positive emotional states through physiological triggers
- *Modeling*: learning to temporarily adopt the behaviors or beliefs of other people whom you see being successful
- *Mental mentors*: creating a team of virtual mentors who can help you work out what to do when you're not sure

Anchoring—Feeling a Strong Response

Most of us have at some time found ourselves responding strongly—and sometimes inappropriately—at an emotional level to an unexpected stimulus. That stimulus can be a piece of music, a particular smell, or even an image or color.

Consciously or unconsciously, the "stimulus" has become what's called a personal *anchor*. Anchors are an everyday part of life. But although they are common, we're often not aware we have them, or of how we acquired them, or of the impact they have on us. *Positive* anchors put us into what is called a *resourceful state*—that is, an intense, can-do feeling that allows us to take action. *Negative* anchors put us into an *unresourceful state* that can lead us to worry about making wrong decisions or stop us from taking any action at all. Managing these anchors in ourselves is critical to building lasting self-confidence. And being able to manage them in others can be a powerful part of our influencing approach.[1]

A successful influencer

- Recognizes how to control his or her own anchors—positive and negative
- Is able to avoid creating or triggering negative anchors in others
- Can create positive anchors in others about his or her cause or case

Negative Anchors

Interestingly, we seem to pick up more negative anchors in our lives than positive ones. And many of these negative anchors are accidentally—or unconsciously—acquired.

You can have a negative anchor about almost anything—even a piece of clothing. For example, you might say to yourself, "This skirt's unlucky—I always get flustered when I wear it." This feeling of "flustered" is probably connected to one time when it rode up at the back and you felt embarrassed in front of the senior team. Now, whether or not the skirt ever rides up again, you feel anxious when you think about yourself wearing it. Interestingly, you may even find yourself tensing when you look in your wardrobe—you're not aware you've seen the skirt, but *subconsciously* the anchor has been triggered.

For most of us, negative anchors have to do with unsuccessful situations in our past. For example:

(*On being invited for a corporate presentation*) "I *hate* meeting in a big boardroom. I get anxious when they're all down at one end of the table. They remind me of when I messed up that big Charity of the Year presentation with Global Corp."

(*If the presentation laptop isn't working*) "I need to have PowerPoint. Every time I've made a presentation without it I've lost us a major donor. Without the presentation I just dry up and can't speak."

(*On being asked to go and talk to a donor over dinner*) "Donor dinners are dreadful. I'm always nervous and end up spilling my wine over the chair of the appeal or some other major donor."

Anchors are often "habitual"—that is, they're built up over time through repeated association. That can make negative anchors difficult to change.

Creating Conscious Positive Anchors

Positive anchors are stimuli that help us get into a more "resourceful" state. Everyday positive anchors include "lucky charms" or talismans. For example, a four-leaf clover, a special tie, or even a particular scent or aftershave are common anchors we use to try and shore up our confidence and create that positive state.

Whereas a particular skirt may have become a negative anchor, a favorite jacket might be one that boosts a resourceful state or feeling: "I always feel more assured meeting difficult donors when I wear this jacket." Of course, the challenge with anchors that rely on *tangible* objects is that you can feel bereft if you lose them. So it's better to learn to create *intangible* anchors from within your own psychological resources.

Figure 6.1 Creating a Positive Anchor

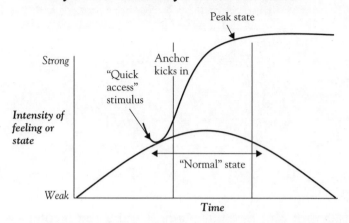

Figure 6.1 shows how an anchor works.

- In your "normal" state you have only a relatively low amount of whatever the feeling is that you want to have.

- It may take you some time to create a higher level of the state you need access to, and you may not have that time.

- By applying an appropriate "quick access" stimulus—the anchor—you set up the response in yourself that you want.

- The anchor creates a higher-intensity feeling or *resourceful* state, which should help to produce a higher performance.

Six Steps to Creating a Resourceful State

Anchoring is simple. But that doesn't mean it's easy. It's a technique you need to practice. The steps in this section will help.

Different situations demand different types of anchored—resourceful—states. So you need to begin by deciding what state you want to reach.

Current State	Desired State
jumpy	calm
bored	excited
nervous	confident
tired	energetic
worried	relaxed

In our work with fundraisers and others we've identified six basic steps to achieving an anchored state. Think of this state as the equivalent of your loading up a new and better mental software program to replace the inappropriate one you've been using. Ideally, you should practice these six steps in a quiet place, free from other distractions.

Step 1: Begin with the end: Ask yourself how you'd like to feel (your state) when you're anchored. Be as *specific* as you can—the more concrete you can be, the better. "Feeling cheerful" may be too vague, and you'll find it harder to get the result you want. Try something more specific, like "feeling enthusiastic and able to energize others." This might be suitable if you want to motivate the volunteers at a make-or-break campaign meeting.

Step 2: Decide on the anchor: What's the specific stimulus you're going to use to anchor your state? Although many stimuli can be used as an anchor—a sound, a smell, and so on—the easiest is usually physical (kinaesthetic). For example, one possibility is touching yourself by squeezing an ear or pressing your fingers together in a particular pattern. The stimulus needs to be different from anything you'd "normally" do. If it is too "everyday"—such as scratching your nose—the danger is you'll either trigger it accidentally or ignore the stimulus altogether because it doesn't stand out for you.

Step 3: Trigger a resourceful state: Recall a real and relevant past experience of being in the emotional and psychological state you want to achieve—when you were successful and felt resourceful. It's very important that it's a *real* experience, but it needn't be *exactly* the same as the situation you're preparing for. Staying with the example of a make-or-break campaign meeting, you might not have been in that situation before, but you *could* recall how you felt when you were able to convince a donor to double their gift, or when you were able to convince that unhelpful hotel manager to upgrade your room when he didn't want to. Bring back the experience as vividly and intensely as you can. Be sure you are *associated*—that is, you're actually in that time, at that place, living that event *from your own point of view*. You may find it easier to close your eyes to do this. Switch on all your senses and listen to what's being said, notice how you feel, see the donor's facial expression. You might even be able to smell the leather of the sofa.

Step 4: "Fire" the anchor: Providing you're fully associated in your resourceful experience you'll reach a peak of intensity. At this point you should apply the physical stimulus or "fire" the anchor you've chosen. You may have to do this for as much as a minute to create a big change in your mental software.

Step 5: "Fix" the anchor: It takes practice to ensure the anchor will create the state you want—be prepared to work at it. This is technically called "fixing" it. To fix an anchor, you need to learn to move quickly and easily between your peak and normal states. So when you've completed step 4, after a minute remove the physical anchor. *At the same time* quickly reduce the mental and emotional intensity of the experience you're re-creating—soften the sound, turn any pictures in your head to black and white, and calm down the feeling. The purpose of this is to help you feel what it's like getting in and out of the state.

Repeat steps 4 and 5 several times until you're confident the stimulus works *and* the state is the one you want. You should also find it easy to get in and out of the resourceful state using and letting go of the anchor.

You may want to do this quickly and in awkward situations. If you've been practicing with your eyes closed, do the same with your eyes open. Try doing it on a bus or in a crowded place as well as in quiet rooms. When you can quickly and easily move from the unresourceful state to the resourceful one you want, you're ready to use the technique "live."

Step 6: Use the state: You're now ready to face your challenging situation. Practice the technique as often as you can. And remember you may need different anchors for different situations—so once you've made the technique work in one way, try some different anchors.

Steve Jobs Can Help You

We've recommended the use of physical (kinaesthetic) anchors because they're easier and require no equipment but your experience. Having said that, music is a wonderfully quick and powerful way to change mood—which makes the iPod a fantastic device for creating anchors. With an iPod you can load up a whole range of different music—songs or instrumental, classical or pop, jazz or blues—to give you access to specific feelings associated with specific music. Aim to have at least one for each key state.

The chart shows a few that we like.

State	Pop	Classical
Confident	KT Tunstall, "Suddenly I See"	Handel, *Zadoc the Priest*
Energized	Queen, "I Want to Break Free"	Beethoven, *Ninth (Choral) Symphony*
Reflective	Lou Reed, "Perfect Day"	Mendelssohn, *Fingel's Cave*

Now think up your own—especially if you hate our taste.

Royal British Legion Anchors

The United Kingdom's Royal British Legion charity has a fabulous anchor in the form of a bright red paper poppy. It is worn on the lapel with a simple pin.

This symbol, bought by and worn by almost all Britons in November each year, is designed to honor the memory of the servicemen and women who have given their lives in past conflicts. The Royal British Legion also uses this anchor as its logo.

It was introduced after the First World War and echoes the fields in Flanders and northern France where poppies grew—and still grow—on the battlefields where millions died. The charity has carefully created a number of specific linked activities to help anchor the memory of the sacrifice:

☐ They organize a two-minute silence nationwide at 11 A.M. on November 11 ("the 11th hour of the 11th day of the 11th month").

☐ For the bigger civic wreath-laying ceremonies they use music such as *The Last Post*.

☐ They hold a remembrance service in the Royal Albert Hall (one of London's largest and most prestigious venues) and at the end drop millions of paper poppy petals from the ceiling.

Not surprisingly, the poppy is instantly recognizable to all Britons, and anchors the remembrance of past conflicts.

Helping Others to Overcome Challenges

As well as anchoring yourself, you can help other people to achieve a more resourceful state. For instance, you may have a colleague who has convinced himself that what he perceives as his "poor" vocabulary will make him look foolish at a donors' reception. You can help him relax.

Assuming you're working with someone who has consciously agreed they want you to help them anchor a particular resourceful state, follow the same six-step model detailed earlier. As their coach, though, it's your job to

- Make sure you have used the technique enough yourself to guide them properly through the process.
- Talk them through the model and its implications, explaining the six steps and how they have worked for you.
- Help them choose an appropriate experience that at least parallels the state they want to achieve.
- Help them choose a suitable stimulus to trigger the anchor—again you may need to help them choose by a process of trial and error.
- Guide them through repeated firing and fixing until they're quickly and easily moving in and out of the desired state.

One word of warning. Do be careful your student doesn't accidentally turn *you* into part of the anchor. Although you might be there at the first presentation, or meeting, or dinner, or whatever, it's no good for either you or the student if you become a walking, talking security blanket.

You'll often see people change physically when you've successfully helped them to achieve a positive anchor or when they've anchored themselves:

- They may breathe more shallowly, deeply, or slowly.
- They may change color, becoming, say, redder as blood goes to their cheeks.

- Their eyes may defocus and they may smile.
- They may seem a bit distant and not respond at first to questions.

These can be helpful signs that they are having a strong "associated" experience. They should come back to "normal" in a few seconds, emotionally refreshed and ready for the challenge they need to face.

Modeling—Be Curious About Others and Learn

Modeling is a way of learning a skill or ability from someone else. First you have to identify a person who is good at the skill or ability you'd like to acquire. Next you need to study the relevant behaviors of that person. And then you adopt these. You may not be able to speak to the person in question—you may want to model someone you have seen speaking at a conference. In that case, the starting point will be to copy the person's body language or physical movements.

The thinking behind modeling is very simple. Our physiology—body language and physical movement—has a big impact on how we feel. If we change our physiology we can change the way we feel. To illustrate this try sitting as though you were feeling miserable. Begin slumped in a chair with your shoulders hunched. Look down. Let your face sag down in a glum fashion. Maybe hold your head in your hands. Staying in that position, now try thinking cheerful thoughts. It's difficult to let them in, isn't it, when your body is sending a "miserable" message to your mind. With modeling you begin by copying observable behavior precisely to experience what messages that behavior then sends to the mind.

You can model famous people. Many people admire Nelson Mandela for his sincerity, for his gravitas, and for his trustworthiness. But how does he convey these hard-to-tie-down qualities? To find out, you need to watch him speaking—get a DVD or watch him on TV. Start by turning down the sound and just look at his body language. You'll notice some distinctive things:

- He moves relatively little—and did so even when he was a young man.
- His lower body is very still.
- He uses his arms and especially his hands for gestures.
- Most of the gestures are within a "box" shape about 2 feet by 2 feet, between his chest and stomach.
- The gestures are all open handed and mostly relate to emphasis on key words.
- He pauses after each gesture.

Now turn up the sound and notice the following:

- He speaks in relatively short sentences.
- He pauses between sentences—and if he's made an important point.
- He has a longer pause after important points to let us absorb the idea.
- He uses his gestures to create a reinforcing element—for example, "This involves all of us" using outstretched open hands.
- He also uses gestures to help change his voice quality—for example, using upward gestures to raise his voice tone and volume at the end of a sentence.

That's a quick analysis of some ways in which Nelson Mandela uses his body to look authoritative, serious, and trustworthy. Apparently he does this day in, day out—even on days when, like the rest of us, he really doesn't feel like standing up there.

So if we adopt behaviors *similar* to Nelson Mandela's, we might appear to have more of these qualities ourselves. And the added bonus is that we get to *feel* more like that too.

You can model almost any skill or aptitude you want. It's not about slavishly copying *every* aspect of someone's behavior. To be successful at modeling you need to begin by identifying an individual who creates an impression or impact that you'd like to replicate. Then you need to be curious about the *key* factors that help them create that impact. If we go back to Nelson Mandela, for example, the key factors are his speech rate and his upper body gestures.

How can modeling be specifically useful in fundraising? It can help you if you identify someone—a colleague, a volunteer, or even a rival—who is good at something you want to be good at. This could be making prospect phone calls, handling complaining donors, chairing meetings, anything. The secret is to follow ten methodical steps:

1. Identify someone who is successful at the skill or ability you want, and check that this is not just *your* impression.

2. Establish what *specifically* it is you want to model (remember you don't want to *be* them—just to model a quality or skill they have).

3. Find an occasion—and ideally more than one—to observe them curiously and carefully.

4. Identify the *behaviors* that contribute to their being successful in this specific area: What do they do and say that's distinctive?

5. Make a note of these behaviors the first time you observe them, and on your second observation see if there's a definite pattern you can establish.

6. Try to identify the three or four key behaviors that make a difference and that you could copy. (You might not be able to copy them all—for example, voice is hard to copy.)

7. Where practical, ask them what *they* think are their secrets.

8. Practice using the behaviors—if you're not sure what are the key ones, try different combinations of voice and action and words.

9. Get someone to observe *you* and tell them what you're trying to do—get them to give you feedback.

10. If you succeed, fine—if not, try modeling someone else *or* some different behaviors from your model.

Mental Mentors—Asking for Help

You almost certainly have people you admire, even if you don't always agree with them—real and imaginary figures from the past, someone from your parents' generation, contemporaries—maybe a selection from all three. You probably admire different people for different things. Wouldn't it be great, then, if you could turn to these people whenever you needed help or advice? If you had a team of *mental mentors*? The good news is you can.

We first heard about this idea in connection with Hillary Clinton during her husband's term of office. As the first lady she was keen to make sure she carefully thought through situations she had to deal with. And her husband was often unavailable for consultation or away on trips. So she invented "mental mentors"—virtual individuals she could trust. She would find herself a quiet space and imagine she was in a discussion with two or more people—historical and contemporary. She would pose some questions on what course of action to take and imagine them advising her on what to say or do. The mentors allowed her to think through the same questions in different ways, opening up alternatives for her to choose from.

The technique is obviously applicable to influence situations and specifically to fundraising tasks when you might not be sure how to proceed. But as you can imagine, it's useful for tackling a whole range of work and personal challenges.

In our own practice we have collected a group of mental mentors to advise us on everything from tactics to choice of

Table 6.1 Possible Mental Mentors

Area for Advice	*Who Might Mentor*
What to say that will move or inspire	John F. Kennedy, Martin Luther King Jr., Shakespeare's Henry V
How to recover from a setback	Thomas Edison, anyone from the crew of Apollo 13, Becky Sharp (from Thackeray's *Vanity Fair*)
What to wear for a specific situation	Paul Smith, Stella McCartney, Donna Karan
How to develop self-confidence	Hermione Granger (from *Harry Potter*), Alexander the Great,[2] Bill Gates
How to stay calm and patient	Dalai Lama, Nelson Mandela, Jane Eyre (from Charlotte Brontës novel)

language to PR initiatives. Of course the answer to what to do really comes from you—or at least from your unconscious. But it's a useful discipline to think about whom you would seek advice from *and* what advice they would offer. It can even give you permission to think the unthinkable.

Table 6.1 shows possible areas for coaching and the kinds of figures—historical and contemporary, real and fictional—who might be able to help you. You can also use people from your own life, of course.

Here are three things to consider when you draw up your list:

- Make sure you choose some people you respect but don't necessarily like. Some of our best advice has come from an imaginary Margaret Thatcher—a person neither of us like politically but who did display great clarity of purpose at various times.

Table 6.2 Authors' Mental Mentors

How to communicate clearly in writing about fundraising	Mal Warwick (U.S. author and consultant), Ken Burnett (inventor of Relationship Fundraising), George Smith (U.K. direct-marketing guru)
How to convey authority and sincerity about the cause	Pierre Bernard Le Bas (former head of fundraising at UNHCR), Per Stenbeck (head of fundraising at UNICEF), Jennie Thompson (the United States' leading campaign consultant)
How to think strategically about the campaign	Hank Rosso (founder of the U.S. Fundraising School), Giles Pegram (director of fundraising at NSPCC), Angela Cluff (an esteemed colleague, deputy director, and principal fundraising consultant at =mc)

- Choose people that you believe you can imagine genuinely speaking to you. Give them a voice. To present you with real choices, they need to appear real to you in your head—probably sitting opposite you at a table.

- Don't feel you need to select people who will agree with one another. It can be useful to have several people who might disagree. That then allows you to weigh options effectively. Remember, it's your choice.

In case you're interested, we've provided a chart with our fundraising mentors (Table 6.2). You may not recognize the names, but they are internationally famous and impressive. Try Googling them.

Once you have your mentoring or coaching group, here's how to use them.

1. Decide the question you want to pose. As ever, it's better to make it as specific as possible. Try to ask questions that might help improve on something. So "How should I challenge that volunteer's behavior?" or "What kind of metaphor or example would make

the biggest impact with that donor?" You can also ask outcome-type questions. For example, "What might be the advantages and disadvantages of writing a follow-up letter to the donor?" Don't ask "yes" or "no" questions. This isn't the I Ching[3] or The Dice Man.[4]

2. Assemble a selection of mental mentors whom you think might be helpful for this specific challenge. Always have at least two and ideally three. Wise people can mentor in different areas. Mahatma Gandhi's ability to mobilize huge numbers of people through peaceful protest—such as the "salt march" campaign—is a great example of a hugely successful and powerful piece of influence. Remember to choose people you don't necessarily like but whose opinion might be useful. And note that your mentors don't *have* to be fundraisers—a businessperson might well be the best person to advise on how to influence another businessperson.

3. Find a quiet space with a comfortable chair where you can think, or fantasize if you like, uninterrupted for fifteen to twenty minutes. Close your eyes and imagine your mentors sitting around a table advising you. Don't try to take notes while being coached.

4. Pose the question to each of your mentors and imagine their answers. Give them time to respond. Imagine them being physically present in the room offering advice. Focus on one mentor at a time. But after you've "heard" the opinion of one mentor it's useful to "look" around the table at the other mentors and seek their views on the advice you've just been offered. In our experience, mentors don't always offer the answer straight away. If they don't know the answer at all then try another mentor. Be open-minded about what you decide until you've listened to all the responses.

5. Open your eyes. And if appropriate take notes on what you heard. If necessary choose between the different options. Remember they're only *mentors*. They're there to

offer advice and help. It's *your* choice about what to do. If necessary you can have one ultimate mentor you can call on to help you make a final decision.

This technique is obviously also useful for dealing with difficult situations like those discussed in Chapter Eleven, "Dealing with Objections."

Summary

Self-confidence is essential in influencing situations. You particularly need it when you have to take on a situation for which you don't feel completely prepared, or in which you've had challenges in the past. Often this lack of confidence is not rational—you have simply had some bad experiences and acquired irrational concerns.

Overall our advice is to find a way to "load up" some better mental software that will help you. The three techniques outlined here are all useful in various ways. A quick summary would be

- If you need a system to develop quick access to a more useful and resourceful state, then try *anchoring*.
- If you want to build up confidence and competence in a specific skill, try *modeling* someone who already has it.
- If you need to think through a complex situation in which you aren't sure what to do, try using *mental mentors*.

Anchoring is the most powerful of the techniques. You can use it in a wide range of situations. When you've practiced it you'll find it can instantly change you from nervous and uncertain to confident and capable. This is also a technique you can use to help others with low self-confidence.

It does, however, require that you methodically follow a six-step approach, and then *practice*. And it asks you to find internal resources—previous success—to tackle the challenge you face.

Modeling is also powerful. It's most useful when you know you need to acquire a new skill or ability but aren't sure how to do it. In modeling you identify someone who has that skill or ability, or even someone who has an impact you want to be able to deliver. Next you literally copy the key parts of their behavior—body language, voice rhythm, and so on. You then see if by modeling their behavior you can have the same impact or effect. When you succeed, you've acquired the knowledge!

Modeling can be difficult, however, if you don't have anyone you can model or it's hard to gain direct access to that person. And you do need to identify what the key behaviors are. It can also take quite a while as you undertake your research and practice.

For more complex issues, when there may not be an obvious answer, we recommend you find some *mental mentors*. The most distinctive feature here is that you are not looking for *one* correct answer straight away. Your mental mentors may each give you very different advice. And you may have to weigh up the pros and cons of their advice carefully. If you've chosen the mentors wisely, they may even give you advice that you really disagree with. But the dialogue between the mentors produces good long-term results.

The key issue is choosing the right mentors. We suggest you assemble a select "A Team" of individuals with different talents and perspectives. Incidentally, we find that historical figures—Joan of Arc, Geronimo, Leonardo da Vinci—can be more useful than contemporary ones. Unfortunately, contemporary mentors sometimes fall from grace!

Notes

1. The origin of anchors comes from the well-established scientific principle of conditioned reflex—that is, the association of a particular response with a specific stimulus.

   The best-known exponent of this idea was Ivan Pavlov. In the early nineteenth century, Pavlov was studying digestion in dogs. He'd observed that the dogs in his experiments would start to salivate when they saw and smelled their food. Then he noticed that the salivation also began when the person who normally brought their food approached carrying a dog bowl, even if the bowl was empty. Pavlov believed this demonstrated a *conditioned* response. To test his theory, Pavlov introduced a completely unrelated stimulus to see if he could still get the same response. He started ringing a bell when the dogs were given their food. He did this a number of times over a period of days. Then he rang the bell when there was no food. The dogs still salivated. He had created a conditioned response. The story of Pavlov's dogs is the story of an *anchor* in action.

2. Alexander the Great? Well, when he started making his great empire he was twenty-one, gay in a very macho society (he was from Macedonia, not Athens), and had no maps of the places he wanted to conquer. What's your challenge?

3. The *I Ching* is a classic Chinese text thought to have originated in the early Zhou dynasty (1122–256 B.C.). It's still used today as a book of divination—or fortune telling.

4. *The Dice Man* is a comic novel first published in 1971 by the American author George Cockcroft under the pseudonym Luke Rhinehart. It tells the story of a psychiatrist who decides to make life decisions based on the throw of dice.

Part Four

Persuasion

7

BUILDING RAPPORT

Our next—and largest—influence cog is *Persuasion*. However, to persuade successfully you first need to build a *connection* to the person you want to influence—the donor, your colleague, a supplier. This connection allows you to understand the way they think and feel, which is essential for other parts of the influence process we discuss in Chapters Eight and Nine. The easiest and quickest way to build a connection is to get *in rapport*. This can be particularly challenging when the person is very different from you, whether it's because of their age, gender, sexuality, faith, or even power and wealth.

In this chapter we look at the skills and approaches that will help you achieve rapport with anyone you need to. The four principles that underpin rapport are

- Seek connection
- Identify commonality
- Share feelings
- Stay in the relationship "flow"

By following these four principles you can ensure that the way you *intend* to come across is the way you *actually* come across.

Finally, we explore body language, voice, and words—the three key channels for transmitting information about ourselves and receiving information from others.

Without rapport you will find it considerably harder to sell yourself, your ideas, or your cause. With rapport the *persuasion* process will be much easier, and you'll gain much greater trust from the donor.

Why Bother with Rapport?

As a fundraiser you have to deal with many people—including prospective and actual donors—who are not like you. They may be businesspeople, whereas you come from a nonprofit background. Or they may be very wealthy, and you have a modest income. They may not share your faith, gender, or age profile. In addition, you may have to deal with these people in challenging situations, such as a busy donor-cultivation cocktail party at which you only have a few minutes to talk, or in a formal high-risk "pitch" with you on one side of the table and the potential sponsor on the other.

To influence such people successfully—whatever the setting—you need to be able to get into rapport quickly. Rapport is often described as a feeling of being "in sync" with the other person. When you're in rapport, it's easier to introduce your ideas and win people over to your cause. This makes the ability to *build* rapport, to create that feeling of trust and understanding when you need it, extremely important in influence generally, and fundraising in particular.

It's important to stress that the techniques we're going to cover build on the *natural processes* we all use to form positive working relationships and friendships. Most of the time in our personal lives we achieve the rapport process *unconsciously*. Our experience in =mc—backed by a significant body of scientific data—suggests you can also develop the ability to *consciously* build rapport.

Using the techniques described in this chapter you can ensure both that you get your message across *and* that the person you're trying to influence feels confident you've understood and valued them and their views.

Manipulative or Professional?

One of the most successful fundraisers we know is an American, Valerie Humphrey. She used to work for a major U.K. heritage charity, the National Trust, most of whose employees are quintessentially English—reserved, conservative, and Conservative. Valerie is every inch a Californian—outgoing, bubbly, and liberal. So at the National Trust she was very "other." Even so, she was very popular with both her staff and the donors, and a hugely successful fundraiser.

We watched her "working" a room full of current and potential donors. Within minutes of engaging an older donor in conversation she had slowed her speech pattern and was matching his deeper voice tone. She calmed down her natural vivacity and kept her gestures to a minimum as she listened to and carefully answered each of his concerns. She then moved on to a younger woman entrepreneur and spoke to her about the business benefits of associating the woman's company with the charity. Valerie's speech pattern sped up—she was excited to tell the entrepreneur about the proposition—she used her hands to illustrate and emphasize her points.

Valerie wasn't being insecure *or* manipulative—she was very skillfully building rapport by adapting her style to mirror and match the communication style of the donors. She was being *professional*.

The Value of Building Rapport

Rapport, from a French word meaning relationship, is useful in a range of settings.

You need rapport in direct *fundraising* settings to

- Deal with a patronizing, or even aggressive, attitude from a corporate sponsor whom you need both to challenge and to keep working with
- Secure a gift from someone very different from you—perhaps a donor from a culture or faith in which you don't know the customs and values
- Take advantage of a chance meeting with a potential foundation funder at a conference—maybe even in an elevator with only five floors to make your point

We also need it in other work settings. For instance, you're in an awkward performance appraisal meeting with a member of your team and want to stress you value *them* but need them to change their *behavior*. Finally, you'll probably find it useful in *personal* settings such as making a good impression on the "other" family at a wedding.

Key Principles Behind Rapport

As noted earlier, there are four key principles behind rapport:

Seek connection: When we meet people we actively seek connections. Think about what happens when you go to a party. You meet people you don't know and you ask their names, what they do, where they work, who else they know at the party, if they like the wine, if they like the music, and so on. All of these are attempts to find connections.

Identify commonality: The connection we feel as part of rapport comes primarily from the identification of commonality or similarity. The commonality can be about a number of things—a similar sense of humor, shared values, shared interests. So in general we find it easier to get on with people who are like us in some way—in age, in gender, in attitudes, in musical tastes, and in beliefs. The challenge for fundraisers, as we've seen, is we are often not at all like the donors we're seeking support from.

Share feelings: It's important to say that being in rapport *doesn't mean agreeing about everything with the other person.* For example, two friends could have a discussion about Harry Potter. One says, "I loved the last book," and the other replies, "You're kidding. I hated it." The first says, "I can't believe it—it's great." And so on. The friends both have strong (though differing) *feelings* about the same subject. The rapport that they're in is focused on the strength of the feeling.

Stay in the relationship flow: It's also important to understand that rapport *is a process, not a state*—you may fall in and out of rapport several times in a single period. Have you ever been to a dinner party and found you don't know the person you're sitting next to, but on talking to them you find you get on really well? Then the conversation dries up, so you talk to the person on the other side of you. And the same happens there, so you go back to the first person. . . . That's rapport as a *process.*

By applying these principles and the techniques in this book, you can avoid "drying up" with an important donor and remain positively engaged for longer.

Times to Avoid Rapport

Because rapport is a sense of connection with someone else, it's not surprising that there are occasions when you *don't* want to be in rapport:

☐ When the attentions of a potential donor or the person you want to influence are inappropriate—they invite you out for dinner then make it clear the purpose is not business

☐ When the views being expressed are offensive and unacceptable—maybe sexist or racist—and you need to signal very clearly that you disagree

☐ When the support or "deal" you're being offered by the sponsor is unacceptable or unethical—they don't seem to recognize this and you need to make it very clear

In these cases and others it's important to be able to break rapport quickly—and to send a message to the other person that they need to change their behavior.

Aligning Your Communication: Three Channels

To build rapport successfully, it's important that we understand how we send and receive information. Unless we choose to tell them, other people can never truly know our innermost thoughts and feelings—and we can't know theirs. The *words* we use make up one primary "channel" by which we transmit and receive information. The other two are *voice* and *body language*.[1]

Consider an example in which the channels work *together*. You get off the plane after a long trip. Your partner is waiting for you as you walk through into the arrivals hall. There's a loud shout of pleasure, and he or she runs toward you smiling, throws his or her arms around you, and says in an excited, happy voice, "You're back! I missed you *so much!*" All the channels are in sync. You know your partner really *is* pleased to see you.

But what if, instead of running gleefully toward you, your partner stands and waits for you to walk to them. He or she looks down as you approach, not making eye contact. And when you reach your partner, he or she gives you a quick peck on the cheek and says flatly, "You're back. I missed you so much." Chances are, you're starting to feel quite anxious. Although the words are positive, the tone of voice and the body language aren't, and you're getting a *mixed message*.

There has been a significant amount of research into the *relative* impact of the different channels. The man who codified what other scientists and social scientists, from Charles Darwin to Irving Goffman, also observed is Professor Albert Mehrabian of UCLA. His research in the 1980s, based on a series of careful experiments, established the *relative* impact of the three channels, as shown in Figure 7.1.

Mehrabian's research is often misquoted and misunderstood, so let's be clear what this does and doesn't mean. It does *not* mean that the words don't count. It *does* mean that we take in and prioritize data from body language and voice. And it *does* mean that when the body language and voice are "out of sync" with them the words can be seriously compromised. So arguably the *most* important channel in the communication—the words—can be compromised because the other two channels have greater *relative impact*.

When you're on the receiving end of this clash, you experience a phenomenon called "cognitive dissonance," in which the voice or body language (or both) undermine or work against

Figure 7.1 Three Channels of Communication

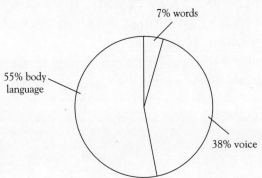

the meaning of the words. Think of the ratios involved. Body language accounts for 55 percent of the communication, voice for 38 percent, and words for 7 percent. That's a ratio of roughly 8 to 5 to 1. So if the words and the body language aren't congruent, the body language is *eight times* more likely to be received than the words. If the body language and voice are *consonant* with the words, the words become incredibly powerful and we experience that person as being sincere. (Depending on the body language and voice, the person could also be perceived as authoritative, angry, relaxed, and so on.)

To make sure your influence message comes across *as you intend*, it's essential that all your communication channels are aligned.[2]

Let Your Body Talk—The Three "M"s of Rapport Building

If body language carries 55 percent of the message in any face-to-face communication, it's clearly the major component in building rapport. And voice, with 38 percent, is not far behind. Think back to that party example. The *words* "Who are you?" or "This red wine is lovely, have you tried some?" are important—they provide the subject. The way you use your *voice*—matching a quiet reflective tone or an excited, high-energy one—is also important: it conveys the mood. But the channel that outweighs both of them in the impression you're making—in building rapport—is your *body language*. If you want to build rapport with donors quickly, start by focusing on matching body language and voice.

It's helpful to distinguish three different levels of activity in rapport building that are often confused:

- Mimicking
- Mirroring
- Matching

Mimicking

Mimicking is *exactly* copying every aspect of someone's body language. We *don't*, under any circumstance, recommend that you use it when you're working to get in rapport with anyone—least of all a donor. The literal copying of body language is likely to be obvious and could make the other person uncomfortable.

But when we're training fundraisers in influence we often start by asking people to "mimic" each other's body language, as it helps them to notice just how much data is transferred in nonverbal communication. This might be useful for you too. We've found that some people are very good at matching upper body posture but fail to notice huge amounts of lower body activity such as a tapping foot. So use mimicking to *learn* but not to *do*.

Mirroring

Have you ever found yourself enjoying a conversation with someone and then noticed that you've unconsciously adopted broadly similar positions? For example, leaning back and laughing at a comment at the same time, or picking up drinks in parallel. This is known as *mirroring,* and is the equivalent of taking a series of behavior "snapshots" of another person's body posture and then *approximating* them. It's basically a good thing to do when seeking to build rapport.

You can see examples of unconscious mirroring all around you. Next time you go into a bar or restaurant take a moment to spot the people who seem to be getting on well. The chances are it's the fact that they are sitting in similar positions or using their hands in a similar way that leads you to that conclusion. They are mirroring each other's body language.

Matching

Matching is the full-color, 3D, real-time movie version of mirroring's Polaroid snapshots. Sometimes called pacing, matching uses body language, voice, *and* words, and involves getting in sync with another person's movements, rhythms, language, and gestures. Because you're using all channels, the impact is richer and stronger.

Again, it's important to stress that matching is a *natural* process—it's something we all do all the time. And like mirroring, we're often completely unaware of what we are doing. When you're standing talking to someone, have you found you both start to gesture at the same time, and even to make the same kinds of gestures? (For example, using a chopping motion with one hand into the other to reinforce points.) Have you ever spent time with someone who has a distinctively different way of speaking from you—maybe their intonation rises at the end of sentences—and found yourself unconsciously speaking like them? Have you found the words or phrases you use are said back to you by other people when you're with them? What you've been doing is *matching* the other person.

There are special challenges in matching body language across genders. Men, for example, will often sit with their legs spread apart. Women in Europe and North America tend not to do this as it's seen as unfeminine. If they match this particular male body language, they are likely to come across as mimicking. In other cultures, however, it's entirely acceptable. In Kenya, for example, you often see women in traditional long-flowing dress sitting with legs akimbo. So for them it can be appropriate to match a man doing the same.

In the following section, we explore *how* you can become excellent at matching. Try to observe it in action, and you'll soon notice how common it actually is. For example, TV chat show hosts often use matching techniques to build rapid rapport with guests. (Notice how Larry King often adjusts his voice to match that of the person he's interviewing.) Interviewers do this to persuade the guest to "open up" about their lives and careers more readily.

What Can You Match? When you match you're choosing to identify and build rapport through a selection of the other person's *behaviors*. The real skill is to identify those behaviors that make the biggest (unconscious) impact on the other person in terms of conveying commonality and similarity.

Some of the main types of behavior you might see are listed in Table 7.1. These behaviors are all significant opportunities to

Table 7.1 Types of Behavior and Matching Elements

Behavior	Elements You Can Match
Posture and body movement	Sitting or standing position—for example, crossed legs or leaning on one leg
	Movement while speaking—for example, leaning forward or back
Gestures	Types of gesture—for example, some people touch themselves for emphasis (this is called a "disclosure" gesture)
	Types of hand gesture—for example, some people "draw" with their hands when talking
Facial expression	Amount of smiling and grimacing plus length of time the expressions are held
	Facial "ticks"—for example, brow wrinkling or lip puckering
Speech rate	Speed at which the person speaks—"normal" is 120 to 140 words a minute, but some people are faster or slower
	Pauses—for example, some people have longish pauses between sentences and you can match these
Voice tone	Intonation and emphasis—for example, rising or falling cadence at sentence end
	Stress on specific words or phrases—for example, "My investment," "This joint *commitment*"
	Pitch—raising or lowering your voice, which may also have an impact on your speech rate; try speaking quickly in a low register or slowly in a high register

match. For example, if you notice the person you're talking to sitting forward, in general so should you—and see if this helps to make the communication easier.

As you become more skilled in matching these behaviors, you'll find you have the chance and ability to observe other, more subtle behaviors (Table 7.2). Matching these can help to take you to very deep rapport. They include

- Breathing patterns—rate and depth of breathing
- Eye contact—amount of gaze and blink rate
- Language—type of language used

Matching Voice Many people are aware of the importance of body language, but voice is often ignored—even though it's up to 38 percent of the relative impact of any communication. Voice matching is particularly important when you're working on the telephone—arranging a solicitation meeting, for example.

Table 7.2 Subtle Behaviors and Matching Elements

Behavior	Elements You Can Match
Breathing patterns	Speed of breathing—fast, medium, or slow Breathing location—high in the chest or lower in the stomach Depth of breathing—lots of shallow breaths or occasional deep ones
Eye contact	Blink rate—how often the person blinks[3] Gaze—whether the person looks at you directly or indirectly Length—how long someone looks at you and the number of times they look away to gather their thoughts, and so on
Language	Visual, sound, or feeling words—for more on this, see Chapter Eight, "Speaking the Language of Influence" Formal or informal language—for example, "Hi" versus "Good morning"

There are a number of elements in voice to consider:

- *Speed*: the rate at which words are spoken
- *Timbre*: the resonant qualities of the voice
- *Volume*: the loudness or quietness of what is said
- *Tone*: the "brightness" of the overall voice
- *Stress*: where the emphasis is in the sentence

Note that voice varies considerably across cultures. For example, in general, Spanish speakers—especially from northern Spain—tend to speak very quickly, whereas Nordics, especially Finns, have a relatively slow speech rate.

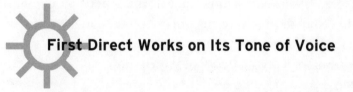

First Direct Works on Its Tone of Voice

There's a U.K. bank that has built its success on being able to match voice elements.

First Direct only does telephone banking. And everyone who banks with the company always comments on how good its customer service is. How does it do this? After all, its interest rates are the same as those of all the other banks; its credit cards are only as useful as any other credit cards; its checks are no more or less valid than any other. So what is it about its customer service that's so good?

The answer is simple. All its operators are trained to match voice tone. If you ring up and ask in a confident, assertive tone to borrow some money for a new car, the operator takes you through the process in a confident, assertive tone. And if you sound anxious and hesitant asking for a car loan, the operator will respond in a quieter, more hesitant tone, all the time taking you through the same process.

They're even trained such that if they call you and you sound like you're relaxed with your feet up on the table, they'll put their feet up on the table in the call center. Or if they catch you when you're walking around the kitchen cooking, they'll stand up, tuck the receiver under their chin like you're probably doing, and talk to you as they pace around the call center.

As a result of this expert voice matching, First Direct is consistently ranked the top bank in the United Kingdom for customer service. We've helped a number of telephone fundraising departments learn from this company and its approach

There's some extra important learning here. Voice quality is often most easily matched by changing your body posture or movement, technically called your *physiology*. By matching someone's physiology you'll find it easier to match their voice. So if the person at the other end of the phone is speaking more quickly than is natural to you, try waving your hand at the same rate like a conductor's baton. You'll find you speed up almost without thinking about it.

Beyond Body Language and Voice

Rapport is not just about body language and voice, though these are very important. It's also possible to match

- *Experiences:* "Wow, that's exactly what happened to me."
- *Skills and talents:* "I play piano too. Isn't it great?"
- *Likes and dislikes:* "Yes, I think that too much cream is sickly."

You can then move on to match at a deeper level through

- *Beliefs:* "Good point, there is too much emphasis on the individual today."
- *Values:* "We obviously agree on the importance of education."
- *Attitudes:* "You're right, the young should be more respectful."

You can be more sophisticated in matching beliefs, values, and attitudes than simply saying the right words—you can demonstrate your real commitment. Table 7.3 offers some examples.

As with body language and voice, you don't want to match *all* the beliefs and values of your donor. Nor is it necessary to become a clone of the other person or to slavishly copy everything they do. The secret, again as before, is to choose a small number to match. Try these and see if you can build greater rapport.

Table 7.3 Commitment in Matching Values, Beliefs, or Attitudes

Value, Belief or Attitude	*How to Demonstrate Your Commitment*
I am trustworthy and reliable.	Ensure that you carry out any action you promise to do.
	Always turn up for meetings or make calls on time.
	Use words like *commitment, promise,* and *certainty.*
I am creative and flexible.	Offer a number of different options or possibilities.
	Encourage left-field thinking from the person or people you're working with.
	Be prepared to change your opinion or decisions when there's reason.
I am principled and value-led.	Share any appropriate values or beliefs you hold.
	Display interest and understanding of others' values and beliefs.
	Avoid any suggestion of compromise on inappropriate issues.

Rapid Rapport

When you want to build rapport with someone quickly there are seven key steps:

1. *Begin with them:* Before you start trying to communicate any ideas or to influence someone, build a relationship by paying attention to them and their preferences and interests. Be *genuinely* curious.

2. *Complement their body language:* Pick up on the pattern of their gestures and how they stand or move. Match these, where appropriate, and notice the effect this has.

3. *Find their signature:* People often have a "signature rhythm"—that is, they'll repeat certain movements (nodding their head, tapping the table). If you can pick this up and match it, you will very quickly build rapport.

4. *Match their communication style:* Notice what type of words or phrases, or even ways of speaking they prefer, and work them subtly into your own communication. (See Chapter Eight, "Speaking the Language of Influence," for more on this.)

5. *Breathe and blink in sync:* This one takes practice! Match their breathing and blink rates. Be careful not to mimic, but if you get it right you'll find it a very powerful bridge to building subtle rapport.

6. *Work with their preferences:* Notice how they like to receive information. Some people like big picture stuff and some prefer details. Others prefer to work *toward* positives and some *away* from negatives. (See Chapter Ten, "Helping Donors Say 'Yes,'" for more on this.)

7. *Review and replay:* Always review the success or failure of your rapport initiative. Look at it in terms of what you planned to do, what worked in practice and what didn't. Use the movie technique and freeze frame your actions to assess them. (Chapter Nine, "Understanding Their Point of View," will offer insights here.)

Rapport Undercover

In the Preface to this book we talked about Caroline, development director of a medical research unit. We explained how she secured the opportunity to make a ten-minute presentation to the Saudi Royal family and their advisers to secure a $25 million donation for her cause. She sought advice from us on how to present the case. Some of the advice we offered was helpful and productive. Some was wide of the mark. The advice she found most helpful concerned the rapport element of the interaction.

There were some big challenges. To be respectful of the status and culture of those she was going to meet, Caroline had to efface herself behind a loose-fitting, full-length dress and headscarf, which meant all that could be seen were her hands and face. How was she to build rapport when denied much of the 55 percent of information from body language? And how was she to do it in just ten minutes wearing a garment that felt completely alien?

We coached her to focus on two specific areas. One was matching the blink rate of each person as she spoke to them. Caroline thought this a little strange but agreed to try. She found it easy with the two women in the group she met. With the men this was harder, but she reported she had matched them as best she could. A second coaching tip was to match the voice pattern and volume of each person who spoke to her. (This also proved hard because much of the conversation was being translated from Arabic. But we had anticipated this and told her to focus on matching the *speakers* rather than the *interpreter*. We wanted her to build rapport with the decision makers, not the interpreter.)

Caroline worked hard to follow our advice. She concentrated on matching the different blink rates of each person as she shared the charity's vision. One individual, she said, seemed like he would never blink as he held her gaze while looking quizzical about the size of the investment she was asking for.

She answered questions at the end methodically. She focused on listening to the questioner and their voice, then taking note of the translation. In her responses she carefully adopted the slower pace of one individual, the fast-speaking pattern of another, and the long, long pauses between phrases of a third in her answers.

The next day she rang us from the airport to say they'd loved her presentation. As important, the interpreter—who dropped her off for her flight—had fed back that he'd been impressed by what he called "her confidence and charm." Most people who presented to the group, he said, failed to make an impact. He could tell they had liked her and her ideas.

The day after, she forwarded the e-mail she had received telling her she'd got the money—and had secured the future of the research unit and its pioneering work.

Leading—Taking Control

There are times when simply matching someone you want to win around to your point of view isn't enough, as they themselves aren't currently in the right frame of mind to agree to your idea or request. They appear tired and disengaged, and you want them to be excited and fired up by your project or idea. If that's the case, you need to take your rapport building one step further and see if *leading* will help.

Leading is when you consciously work to *change* the other person's state or perception. It's useful when you want that person to understand the world from *your* perspective or change their behavior. Whatever your purpose, you need to begin with rapport. Don't try to lead someone to a new state *before* you've spent time matching where they are now. The rule is simple: *in order to change someone's view of the world you first have to enter into their world.*

The rule of three applies to leading. That is, you'll most likely need to match three behaviors before you've achieved a high enough level of rapport to be able to lead. If you're not at the right level of rapport, the other person is much less likely to follow.

You normally lead by changing some aspect of your body language, for example, if you've been *matching* a donor's relaxed position by sitting back, breathing deeply, and speaking slowly. You're in rapport. But you don't want to match their spoken perception that there are many challenges to consider with the fundraising campaign.

You now want to *lead* and get them excited and engaged. So you lean forward and offer a positive affirmation of something positive they've said and stress, "That's a good point." You continue, "I wonder, then, if you'll be interested in the community

Figure 7.2 Matching to Lead

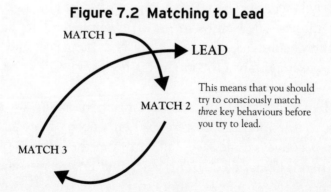

This means that you should try to consciously match *three* key behaviours before you try to lead.

hospice project we're running that answers that challenge." See if they move forward to adopt something closer to your position.

If they do—you're *leading* and you've succeeded. If not, you need to match and pace them some more. If the behavior you've matched isn't enough then try matching a different behavior, such as their voice tone or their language pattern. Then have another go at leading them to a more engaged state.

Leading can also be a useful technique in job interviews. When the interviewee arrives, he or she may be feeling nervous. Giveaways about this can be the interviewee speaking quickly, moving awkwardly, leaning forward anxiously, and clasping and unclasping their hands. By leaning forward yourself, matching the speed of their speech, and clasping and unclasping your hands you'll match their anxiety and build rapport. But in this case you don't want them to *stay* nervous—you want them to relax.

So after a few minutes of such matching you comment on how interesting some answer they've made is and smile. Then you lean back in your chair and adopt a slower speech pattern that you think might help them to become more relaxed. If they respond, and also lean back and smile, you've succeeded.

Summary

People communicate through three main channels: words, voice, and body language. The relative impact of these channels is one of the most studied ratios in social psychology. The channels with the greatest *relative* impact are body language and voice. Words are important for content or the *information* we're trying to convey.

When these channels are working in harmony we appear honest, authentic, and sincere. When one or more of these channels conveys a message different from the other two—say, shaky hands alongside a strong voice and upbeat message—we can appear inconsistent or dishonest. This phenomenon is known as *cognitive dissonance*.

It's easier to win people over to our point of view when we're in rapport. Rapport is a sense of trust and responsiveness between you and another person.

Building rapport involves matching a careful selection of behaviors from within the three communication channels to demonstrate to others that you're in tune with them. This is a *natural* process that we can become good at in a conscious way. Once in rapport, we become more effective at influence.

We can build rapport simply to help transmit our message more clearly. We may do it to help lead someone to understand, accept, and act on behalf of our cause. When you want to build rapport quickly there are seven key steps:

1. Begin with them
2. Complement their body language
3. Find their "signature"
4. Match their communication style
5. Breathe and blink in sync
6. Work with their preferences
7. Review and replay

Just as matching is a useful way to build rapport, *dispacing* is useful when you want to deliberately break rapport. You can dispace by *mismatching* body language, voice, or language.

Finally, once you have rapport you can *lead:* that is, change someone's state or attitude by introducing a more positive piece of body language accompanied by a positive verbal reinforcement.

Notes

1. These three channels transmit two kinds of data. The first provides the surface content of the communication—I like you, I need your help, I'm worried, and so on. The second is the basis on which we form some fundamental views about

the person: are they being truthful, do they feel confident, can they be trusted, and so on.

2. The relative importance of each channel is altered when the communication is not face-to-face. For example:

- When you talk to someone on the telephone you can't see them, so words and voice become more important. But if you listen carefully you'll find you can "hear" a smile or a frown in their voice tone—which is why telesales people often have a mirror in front of them when they're making a call.

- When you e-mail someone, the *only* channel is the words, so naturally they acquire an extremely high level of importance. (That's why emoticons—:), :O, :(, and so on—can be helpful in e-mails or in instant messaging. They allow you to show you're being ironic or humorous.) The skill then is to find a way to inject the right "tone of voice."

By clever and sensitive use of written language we can encourage a reader to replay a voice in their head, or even to call a picture to mind. This is especially important in distant or remote communication.

3. Hypnotists work initially by developing rapport and then leading. (See later in this chapter for a discussion on *leading*.) If you watch their technique, typically you'll see they often start by asking someone to relax. Then they focus on *matching* a person's blink rate—so they'll say, "You feel . . . sleepy" and use the word *sleepy* as the subject blinks. Then they wait until the subject blinks again and on the blink say, "Your eyes feel t-i-r-e-d" and so on. This reinforcement of a *natural* behavior begins the process of *leading* into a state like a light sleep. And when the eyes finally remain shut the hypnotist has succeeded in putting the subject into a trance.

8

SPEAKING THE LANGUAGE OF INFLUENCE

This chapter is designed to challenge your current perception about how donors and others use language. It is also designed to help you become a better fundraiser by developing greater flexibility in the way *you* use language—paying attention to your own and others' preferences.

We introduce a framework called Neuro-Linguistic Programming (NLP), originally developed from an academic study of high-achieving professionals. The flexibility of these professionals in using language proved to be a key determinant of their success.

Linguistic flexibility is an essential complement to the flexibility in body language and voice explored in Chapter Seven, "Building Rapport."

Specifically we look at

- How we adjust the words we use to share ideas in a way that others will find more acceptable
- How the kinds of words other people use help us to understand how they think

Why Some Professionals Have More Success

In the early 1970s two academics at the University of California, Santa Cruz, began a study of different professionals who were outstandingly successful in their chosen careers—salespeople, lawyers, and therapists. John Grinder, a linguistics professor, and Richard Bandler, an undergraduate specializing in computer programming, were interested in what made these professionals truly excellent. Their question was, "Why, with the same qualifications and experience as their peers, did some professionals achieve significantly better results—greater sales, higher acquittals, more 'cures'?"

Bandler and Grinder interviewed and videotaped their subjects. The research established that the professionals used—unconsciously or consciously—a number of the techniques discussed elsewhere in this book. For example, they were good at building rapport through body language and voice. But for these individuals to be as successful as they were, there had to be some *additional* level of skill.

Eventually the researchers identified the additional skill from a detailed linguistic analysis of video transcripts they made of their subjects in action. Their subjects didn't only match the *body language* and *voice* of the person they successfully influenced, they also changed their own *spoken language* to match as well. It was this *extra* factor that made the difference. From this initial discovery Bandler and Grinder developed a body of work now called Neuro-Linguistic Programming (NLP).[1]

Put simply, NLP tells you that by paying attention to the words a person uses, you can gain essential information on how to best communicate with—and so influence—that person.

For us as consultants, NLP is a key tool we use in coaching fundraisers in high-level asks. We also use it specifically to improve the impact of case statements. (See Appendix C, "Translating Your Case," for a worked example.)

Speaking the Same Language—Sensory Systems

Bandler and Grinder's work established that individuals tend to use language that reveals their preference for how their brain is gathering and processing information. These preferences are referred to in NLP jargon as *sensory systems* or *sensory modalities*.

Let's try an experiment to establish your preference—or preferences—for different sensory systems. Take a minute to think about a meal in a restaurant you've had that you really enjoyed. Pause to recall this real situation for a moment and notice what comes to mind:

- Is it a picture of the beautifully presented food, the sparkling glasses and cutlery, and the different colored tea lights on each table?

  or

- Is it the smell and taste of the food, the feel of the crisp ironed tablecloths, and the pleasure of being in great company?

  or

- Is it the curious choice of muzak, the odd restaurant-language used on the menu, and the clatter of pots and pans as the kitchen door swings open?

You *may* have recalled all three with equal intensity. But more likely you remember one sensory experience much more strongly than the others. The strength of that recall provides an insight into your preferences. (Even if they all appeared to be equal, the *sequence* they came in can help reveal your preference.)

Essentially there seem to be three main choices in how people take in, organize, and express information—as pictures, feelings, or sounds. In NLP-speak these three primary sensory systems are as follows:

- *Visual*: perceiving and expressing ideas primarily in pictures, images, colors and shapes. Such a person might ask for "Some clarification on what your organization's strategic focus is."

- *Auditory*: perceiving and expressing ideas primarily through sounds and words. Such a person might ask for "Time to spell out what the organizational objectives say about your strategy."

- *Kinaesthetic:* perceiving and expressing ides primarily through feelings, touch, taste, and smell. Such a person might ask for "The chance to get a handle on what you're keen to push ahead on strategically."

Bandler and Grinder's research showed that the "added extra" their exceptional professionals had was *the ability to unconsciously identify and match another person's sensory language preference.* Moreover, these high achievers were able to switch into another's language style quickly and easily, and it was this ability that was largely responsible for their exceptional level of influencing success.[2]

It's important to stress, however, that although most people have a *preference* for one of these systems when they're communicating, everyone can *access* all of them.

How Specifically Can NLP Help You Fundraise?

NLP has developed over the years with many extraordinary claims made about it, especially concerning personal development. We're not going to explore those. The essential benefits of NLP to fundraisers are simple:

- ☐ It shows you how to *build rapport* through *language* with very different or even difficult donors quickly and easily. It helps you to do this genuinely and authentically through curiosity.

- ☐ It gives you an understanding of *why donors and even colleagues use words differently* from you and why these differences may create objections to your fundraising proposition.

□ It also shows you how to deal with these concerns, if they do arise, in a systematic and practical way.

□ It allows you to understand how *best to express your case*—adapting your language and presentation style to ensure that the fundraising message you transmit arrives effectively and as you intended.

Let's consider the three systems in a little more detail.

The Visual Person

If you primarily use the visual system, you notice first what you *see*. You organize and remember your thoughts in images or pictures. As you talk you explain that you *see* challenges ahead, you plan to *focus on* priorities, and you want to *look at* the *big picture*.

At a work meeting you might notice the shape of the room, the mark a coffee mug has left on the table, and the curiously shaped earrings of the woman chairing the meeting. Afterward you can picture where people were sitting and how they were sitting—leaning away from or into the group—and the diagram someone drew on the whiteboard.

In a fundraising context you may need to sketch out the priorities for the visual donor, help them to get an overview of your organization, look through some different options for future support, and show them photographs of the new building being used by beneficiaries that their donation has helped to open. Notice here how the references are to interaction through *pictures and images*.

The Auditory Person

If your primary system is auditory, you first take in and organize information by what you *hear*. You might find yourself replaying arguments or speeches in your head, rehearsing your responses to difficult donor questions, and generally talking things over with yourself. When you explain things to someone you may finish by saying, "Does that *sound* right?"

At a work meeting you might find that the office noise outside the room makes it hard to concentrate, and, wondering where the person with the unusual accent is from, you only half hear the chair's summary of agreed action. Remembering the meeting, you may recall parts of the conversation verbatim and the tone of heavy sarcasm in the voice of one of your colleagues when they were asked to sum up the situation.

In a fundraising setting you might offer to spell out the organizational priorities to an auditory donor, to explain the case without using gobbledygook or jargon, to talk through different options for future support, and to share written case studies in which beneficiaries explain how they've gained from your help. Notice here how the references are to interaction through *sounds and words*.

The Kinaesthetic Person

If your preference is the kinaesthetic—or feeling—system, you're likely to notice physical sensations when you first enter a room, such as the temperature and the smell—of air freshener, if it's used, or paper, or leather furniture. You may also be attuned to the emotional content of any situation. When you explain things, you talk about tackling the *tough issues first*, *ironing out* the poor bits of a presentation, or *working hard* to get on with someone.

At the work meeting you might notice how warm the room is and how uncomfortable the chairs are. Remembering the meeting you may recall how frosty the discussion got at a particular point and how it made you feel on edge. But the pastries, you recall, tasted delicious. . . .[3]

With a kinaesthetic donor you'll stress that you know you're asking for a challenging gift, and that your cause has recently made some tough choices, and that beneficiaries responded warmly to the help the donor's generous donation provided.

Notice here how the references are to interaction through *feelings and physical interaction.*

Working with Language in a Fundraising Case

Later in this chapter we deal with the issue of working with donors "live" in a conversation or in a presentation. But to improve your skills in switching systems you'll probably find it easier if you practice working on a written case—a formal explanation of your cause and need for money. (See Chapter Four, "Making Your Case," for the structure and purpose of a case.)

In our work with clients we've used this NLP language model to tailor donor-specific cases—or fundraising propositions—specially to match the sensory preferences of an individual. The payoff is they're instantly more understandable and more acceptable to that individual.

It's as important and as respectful to translate your case into different system preferences as it is to translate your case into Spanish or Chinese for non-English-speaking donors.

When you're writing a *general* case aimed at a range of donors you need to write it in a "rich" way that uses *all* the modalities. You can use this approach in other influence settings. Imagine a speech by a CEO to her colleagues:

"We've had some challenging returns against budget for the last fiscal period. And these have created some medium-term challenges for our services—especially with regard to service programs. Please be aware of the implications of these constraints on our cash flow and ultimately on the financial viability of the helpline service. Take appropriate action to avoid unnecessary expenditure or to minimize it where practical."

Now imagine the same speech using the principles of richer communication:

"I have to tell you we've made a significant loss in the last three months, with income well below our fundraising projection. Those red numbers you can see at the bottom of the budget mean we're all going to have to tighten our belts in the next three to six months. Let me say it really clearly. Everything you buy has to be paid for. If we can't sign the checks to keep things going, that could mean phones ringing unanswered on the helpline. Whenever you can, don't spend money—beg or borrow, or at least ask colleagues if there's a cheaper way to do it."

Which of these speeches conveys the information more clearly?

Unequal Preferences

Not all the NLP language preferences are evenly distributed. Recent research suggests that

- [ ] 35–45 percent of people have a predominately *visual* preference.
- [ ] 25–35 percent of people have a predominately *kinaesthetic* preference.
- [ ] 5–15 percent of people have a predominately *auditory* preference.

Other interesting data includes:

- [ ] There are no significant cultural differences worldwide—so these distributions seem to hold in places as different as Africa and America.[4]
- [ ] There are no differences in gender—so women are not, as you might imagine, more kinaesthetic than men.
- [ ] Some professions have higher densities of the styles— there are more auditory people in IT and finance.

How to Notice a Donor's Preference

Most people, including donors, don't communicate *exclusively* in one preference—what we're looking at (or talking about, or getting a feel for) is *frequency* of language.

Below we've started a list of typical words and phrases that could provide you with cues for when someone is using each system. You should be able to add to it. But notice that you will probably find it easier to add to one or two of the lists because of your own preferences.

Visual system: typical words include look, picture, focus, imagine, visualize, reflect, perspective, clarify, hazy, dim, color

Auditory system: typical words include say, accent, ring, clear, discuss, remark, silence, tell, volume, sound, resonate, articulate

Kinaesthetic system: typical words include touch, handle, contact, rough, sensitive, stress, touch, grasp, bitter, smell, taste, impact

Visual: typical phrases include we see eye to eye; I see what you mean; you have a blind spot; at first glance; looks pretty good to me; showing the way forward; future looks brighter

Auditory: typical phrases include on the same wavelength; that rings a bell with me; listen to yourself talk; a quick chat through; music to my ears; calling the tune; talking up the future

Kinaesthetic: typical phrases include really connected; that fits with my feeling; you're stuck on that idea; scratch the surface; control yourself; sweet smell of success; feeling good about the future

Remember that everyone uses a mix from all the systems[5]—what you're looking for is a *preference*. So an auditory donor will simply say more words or phrases from that cluster—giving you a clue to their preference.

Preferences at Cross Purposes

Chris is a very successful fundraiser. He is also very kinaesthetic. So he cares passionately about his cause and tends to work off of a gut response with donors, sensing how they feel. His primary concern is to relax the donor and then work through any challenges. He hates going to prospect meetings with Jan. Jan is way too auditory. She always wants to rehearse their arguments beforehand. And she insists they divide up who will answer which question if the donor asks it. She takes lots of documentation with her, determined to have access to all the facts in response to any quibble.

One day they both have a dreadful meeting with a donor, Alan, who insists they clarify their budget and show him the difference his gift could make. He can't see how he fits in to the organizational picture. (Alan prefers visual.)

Alan, Chris, and Jan probably don't have any fundamental disagreements. They probably all want to achieve the same thing. But they are struggling to even *begin* to communicate because each is working exclusively in their own sensory preference and not being very flexible.

How to *Quickly* Assess a Donor's Preference

You may be concerned that you'll find it hard to pick up a donor's preference. Or you may worry that you'll find it hard to assess their preference *and* concentrate on the content of your message at the same time.

Fear not. The answer is to focus on discovering the donor's preference *before* you get to the *important* part of the discussion. Use the "ice breaking" time at the start of any meeting or phone call to good effect. Classic conversation openers like "How are you?" "How was your journey?" "Did you have a good holiday?" and so on, are not simply idle chatter. For the excellent influencer, it's a critical time for gathering key information about the donor.

For example, visiting someone in their house and being shown into their study, you can start a conversation by remarking, "This is a great study!" Notice that their response will often take one of three forms:

"Thank you. I love the view of the garden from here, and I find I can bring real clarity to my thought." (visual)

"Thank you. It's quiet here with the garden and no traffic—so I can hear myself think." (auditory)

"Thank you. I get the scent of the flowers when it's warm, and when I want a break the garden helps me to relax and sort out what's really important for me to get to grips with." (kinaesthetic)

Even before you step into someone's office or home, you can pick up valuable information. Read an e-mail they've written giving you instructions on how to find them. Again, you'll notice some differences in the way people give directions:

"We're opposite the bank on the corner. There's a parking lot entrance on the left, though you may have to look hard for a parking space. As soon as you walk back out of the parking lot you'll see our bright red 'Big Co' sign." (visual)

"We're near a very noisy bar. Ask the parking attendant to tell you where there's a parking space if you have to. The words 'Big Co' are on the wall in red nearby—they caused a lot of comment when they were put up—that's where we are." (auditory)

"It's not an easy place to find—and sometimes the parking lot is crowded. But everyone knows our offices, and the red 'Big Co' sign is a sure way to guide you through the confusion." (kinaesthetic)

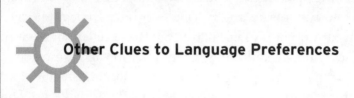

Other Clues to Language Preferences

Apart from the words that people use, there are other clues to a person's preferences you can look for. For example:

☐ People who are *visual* tend to speak quickly, use a lot of gestures, and breathe shallowly and in the upper part of their bodies.

☐ People who are *auditory* often have very even or melodious voices and breathe evenly with few gestures—though they often "tap" in rhythm as they speak.

☐ People who are *kinaesthetic* are likely to speak more slowly, with pauses between ideas. They look down a lot as they speak and breathe from the bottom of their stomachs.

For more on these clues and especially on how eye movement can help you, see Appendix A, "Accessing Eye Cues."

Curiosity and Flexibility

It's easy to think of NLP as merely a way to analyze people and make quick judgments about them. But to be really skillful in using it, and to build rapport generally, you need to be genuinely *curious* about people. This involves not only noticing their preferences but also how and when (and in what circumstances) they change their preference. It's only then that you can begin to build *language rapport* with them, to balance your body language and voice rapport (see Chapter Seven, "Building Rapport").

Being curious also helps you to take the time to determine that your idea or proposition has arrived with the prospective donor in the way you intended, and that they fully understand it.

Three Key Skills

A curious person is one who's openly and constantly searching for information about others. If you're a truly curious person, you'll begin by being curious about *yourself*: "Why did I do that?" "How do I know that?" "Why do I think that?" And you'll begin to notice why you have certain kinds of preferences and how these affect the way you work, think, and make decisions. It's then easier to be curious about others.

Apart from general curiosity, you need access to *three key skills* to be successful in building language rapport:

☐ *Diagnosis:* This is the ability to *accurately* understand and analyze another person's preferred way of thinking and communicating—their "style." Remember this is not the same in every situation—so you need to notice changes.

☐ *Flexibility:* It's not enough just to know what someone's style is. You've got to be flexible enough to change and adapt your own style and approach to match theirs. And you have to be able to do it skillfully.

☐ *Outcome:* You need to know what you want as an end result in any given situation—a donation, a new perspective, an agreement to a change. The more specific the outcome the more easily you can direct your language.

To be a really successful fundraising influencer, you need to develop your flexibility with the systems that are outside your own preference, and be able to use them in "live" situations. This is much the same as a top tennis player practicing on different surfaces in order to be able to adapt his or her game to play on grass or clay. The secret, as always, is practice!

You can develop your flexibility in a number of ways:

- Listen to the radio or the TV carefully and with curiosity. Notice who speaks in one of the systems almost exclusively and who swaps between them. Often people speaking "off the cuff"—that is, taking part in live reporting or impromptu interviews in which the interviewee is not choosing their words very carefully—can display a preference very strongly. Notice how quickly you can spot changes.

- Set yourself the exercise of translating the same speech with the same message to three people in an audience who each uses one system exclusively. Imagine each is a commercial sponsor and you need to explain the benefits of supporting your charity concert. How might you share a benefit, such as brand awareness, in the three systems? ("Can't you just see your company name up there in lights?" "Won't you feel proud at the connection of your company's logo with a joyful evening?" "Can you hear the applause and people talking about what a great company you are?")

- Choose an object, such as a car, or a flower—or a fundraising technique, such as a bequest or a direct mailing. Without mentioning exactly what it is, describe its characteristics in one sensory system to someone, while they try to guess what it is. How difficult is it if you're not using *your own* preferred system? Was it easier for them to guess what it was when you used *their* preferred system?

Over time you'll find that switching "live" between systems becomes easier—but, as we've said, it takes practice.

How Do We Communicate with Lots of People at Once?

The discovery that people have preferences for different systems has implications for all one-to-one fundraising and influencing. But how do you deal with a big crowd—such as a conference or a pitch to a corporate board—in which there are lots of people, all with their own preferences? You obviously don't have time to go around asking each of them questions and responding in their preferred modality.

The answer is you have to learn to use all three systems at once.

Many inspiring communicators do this naturally. Martin Luther King Jr. understood *unconsciously* how to communicate his message to every one of 250,000 civil rights protesters. It was 1963—well before Bandler and Grinder's research.

"'We hold these truths to be self evident; that all men are created equal.'" (auditory—Dr. King is consciously quoting from the Declaration of Independence.)

"... the red hills of Georgia ..." (visual)

"... a desert state sweltering with the heat of injustice and oppression ..." (kinaesthetic)

Martin Luther King's speech ensures that every sense is stimulated:

- It paints pictures and draws images.
- It asks us to hear the voices of others.
- It appeals to our sense of smell and of taste and to our feelings.

Dr. King made sure he communicated with—influenced—*everyone* in the crowd.

This skill goes even further back. Consider the following quotation from Shakespeare's *Henry V*. It's the untried boy king's rallying cry on the eve of the Battle of Agincourt. He has to inspire *all* the troops to follow him against an exceptionally strong enemy. And to do that, he has to engage all the sensory systems and deliver his rallying cry in a way that touches and engages even his most world-weary and cynical soldiers.

> "This day is called the Feast of Crispian. (auditory)
>   He that outlives this day and comes safe home (kinaesthetic)
>   Will stand a-tiptoe when this day is named
>   And rouse him at the name of Crispian. (kinaesthetic and auditory)
>   He that shall see this day and live t'old age
>   Will yearly on the vigil feast his neighbors (visual and kinaesthetic)
>   And say, 'Tomorrow is Saint Crispian.' (auditory)
>   Then will he strip his sleeve and show his scars (visual)
>   And say, 'These wounds I had on Crispin's day.'" (auditory)

You have probably noticed that great writers and orators through the ages have used this technique unconsciously. The good news is that, thanks to NLP, *we* can now use it—maybe not as skillfully, but still with purpose.

Summary

Research has demonstrated that high achievers in many fields partly owe their results to the quality of their communications skills. The research has been codified in a framework called Neuro-Linguistic Programming (NLP.)

This framework suggests that the pattern of words you use offers an insight into how the brain, your bio-computer, is processing and storing information. It establishes that there are three main language preferences or sensory systems that individuals use to communicate. These are

- Visual—mostly pictures and images
- Auditory—mostly sounds and words
- Kinaesthetic—mostly feelings and touch

Everyone has access to all three systems, but most people have a preference for one or two.

As a fundraiser and influencer you have to be *curious* to be effective—first noticing other people's linguistic preferences and then being flexible enough to match them. By swapping between these you can communicate with all kinds of donors and colleagues. And if you communicate more effectively you're more likely to be able to influence.

Any fundraising proposition or case for support is most likely to be written—initially—in the system or modality preferred by the writer. The person who has to receive and act on the information—for example, the donor—may not share the same preference. So for a case to be successful with the widest possible audience it needs to be "translated."

- If you're going to be with a specific individual you'd like to influence, you need to make sure your message is targeted in a way that directly appeals to them.

- If you're going to present your ideas to a number of individuals you'd like to influence, you need to make sure your message is created in all three systems to achieve maximum reach.

Great authors have always done this, so we can learn from them. But for mere mortal fundraisers, the secret is *practice*.

Notes

1. *Neuro* refers to the idea that the way we gather and interpret information is a function of neurological (brain) processes—taste, touch, smell, feeling, sight, and hearing. Although everyone uses all of these to some degree, most people have a clear "hardwired" preference for one or two. *Linguistic* refers to the fact that our language—the frequency with which we use specific kinds of words and phrases—gives

a clue to the preferences we have for this neurological process-ing. By listening carefully to the kind of language someone uses you can gain an insight into the way they think.

Programming is the idea that although individual *brain pref-erences* are hardwired, we *can* adapt. These adaptations are like mini-additions to the programs in the brain's bio com-puter. (Imagine you have a computer with PowerPoint but not Word. To read the Word document you need to upload the right program. So having preferences different from those of your donor needn't mean you can't communicate suc-cessfully with them—you simply need to "upload" their preferences.)

2. Sometimes the system we favor is influenced by what we're doing or when we're doing it. For example, we're more likely to experience a painting *visually* in the first instance. But our response—or the way we *recapture* or *recall* that experience later—may reflect less about what was illustrated on the canvas and more about how it made us "feel" or what the art-ist was "trying to say."

3. Smell (*olfactory*) and taste (*gustatory*) are often included within the kinaesthetic system because they are both strong experiences that produce strong feelings. For instance, is there a smell from your childhood—such as your mother's perfume—that even just a whiff of today would still bring back strong emotions for you?

4. We've used NLP in our influence and fundraising training in Ethiopia, Kenya, South Africa, Australia, New Zealand, the United States, Canada, Mexico, Brazil, Argentina, Peru, Germany, France, Holland, Sweden, Italy, Thailand, and Malaysia. It seems to work everywhere, and our own experi-ence reinforces the general distribution data given here.

5. Some words and phrases don't really fit into this model, either because they don't have a preference attached to

them or you can't identify one. Such language is called *digital*. Examples would be words such as analyze, answer, communicate, remember, system, use. Also, some phrases are simply clichés and don't reflect a real sensory choice. Examples might include "I hear what you say" or "Back to basics."

9

UNDERSTANDING THEIR POINT OF VIEW— PERCEPTUAL POSITIONS

In this chapter we explore the proposition that in order to *change* someone's point of view, you first have to *understand* it. Specifically, we explore a powerful tool called *perceptual positions*. This tool is an essential part of the *Persuasion* cog in our 5Ps model.

Perceptual positions are important in influence because

- People will experience the same situation from one of three—and sometimes even four—perspectives.
- Each of the perspectives has different strengths and weaknesses from an influence point of view.
- Most people will make a judgment or change their minds more easily in one of these perspectives.

If you become skillful in understanding and adopting the different positions yourself, you'll quickly and easily be able to analyze the best perspective to win someone over.

Positioning for Fundraising Influence

When we watch a movie or TV drama we're used to seeing the action from different points of view. Directors such as Paul Haggis with *Crash* (2004) and Pete Travis with *Vantage Point* (2008) are exemplars. In *Crash* we're shown the individual experiences that occurred before the multi-car accident that brings all the characters together. It's these experiences that explain—if not excuse—the responses of the different characters. In *Vantage Point* we see the same event—the attempted assassination of President Ashton—through the eyes of eight different people.

By taking this approach, Haggis and Travis not only help us understand the motivation of their characters at different points in the action, they also lead us to experience a moment of sympathy for an unattractive or even villainous character. We can appreciate how one situation or event could be interpreted differently according to different perspectives. The same is true in influence.

So it's an essential skill for any successful fundraiser to understand the donor's point of view. It might also help if you could understand the points of view of the donor's partner, financial adviser, children, and any others who may be critical in the donor's deciding whether or not your cause should be supported. As a fundraiser, being able to switch between perceptual positions can open the door for you to

- Frame a fundraising proposition in a way that appeals to the donor
- Anticipate likely objections and possibly prepare answers
- Understand why people give feedback the way they do
- Make better use of the feedback you get
- Recognize what you could have done better when reviewing what happened

Choose Your Position

In our experience there are three *main* perceptual positions that are important in fundraising influence. (There is also a fourth that is useful in some very specific situations, and so we explore this at the end of the chapter.)

Position 1: The Way You Experience the World   In Position 1 you take in and prioritize information through *your* eyes, ears, and emotions (Figure 9.1). In our movie analogy it's as though you are the camera, experiencing any situation from your own perspective.

Figure 9.1

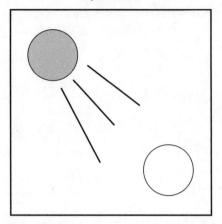

Position 1 is important not just in terms of *perception*—it's also where you hold your values, beliefs, and experiences. So by implication it is also where you hold your prejudices.

At its most appropriate, by being clear about Position 1 you can identify what exactly it is that *you* want in any given situation and be assertive about your needs and interests. At its worst, a perspective wholly based on Position 1 is self-centered and selfish, taking no account of anyone else's concerns.

Fundraisers at their best feel absolutely sure about their cause and its importance in Position 1. At their worst they may not spot that the donor isn't the slightest bit interested in either the work or the proposition.

Position 2: The Way Someone Else Experiences the World
From Position 2 you can step into the other person's shoes and gain an insight into *their* perspective—their needs, wants, values, experiences, and desires (Figure 9.2).

Try going into Position 2 to help you understand why you're not "connecting" satisfactorily to someone, or to identify why that person feels something is important that doesn't seem at all important to you.

Figure 9.2

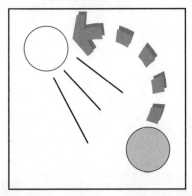

But you need to be careful. If you become completely immersed in Position 2 you can identify too strongly with the other person and their interests, losing your sense of self and holding back too much on your needs—the needs of your cause.

Fundraisers at their best can use Position 2 in a number of ways. It can help them to identify strongly with the *donor*—understanding how to frame the ask, empathizing with how big a commitment the donor is making, and even appreciating how they should dress when they make the solicitation. Those same fundraisers might also appreciate and be able to share powerfully the point of view of the *beneficiaries* of the solicitation, accurately sharing the feeling of isolation experienced by the young homeless person they are seeking funds to help. At their worst, a fundraiser using Position 2 might back away from the solicitation because he or she senses this gift might cause a row between donor and adviser or partner. Or the fundraiser may get too involved in the perception of the homeless person and their needs and become over-emotional—losing the sense of perspective offered by emotional intelligence (see Chapter Two).

Position 3: Observing the Interaction from an Objective "External" Position   In Position 3 you step out from any *internal* perspectives—yours or theirs (Figure 9.3). (James Ury, in his book *Beyond Yes or No*, calls this perspective viewing from "the balcony"—looking down on the action in a detached way.)

Figure 9.3

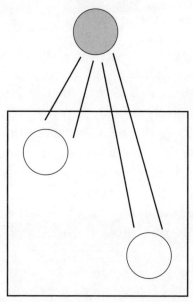

This detached position lets you weigh up both points of view in a situation and maybe decide which has the stronger merit, or where a compromise goal might be reached. Such detachment can sometimes also have a downside, such as being unable to decide either way about an issue, or seeming a little too distanced from feelings or emotions that are present and important.

Fundraisers at their best in Position 3 may be able to almost take "time out" in the middle of a difficult meeting and assess how things are going. They may be able to give themselves advice on how to proceed. With practice they can even replay the "movie" review of what went well or less well in a donor meeting and draw out some learning points for themselves.

At their worst they may appear alienated both from the donor and their own work. This can come out as world-weary cynicism, or "going through the motions." If you find this happening, go back to Chapter Two and reengage with your own passion for the cause.

It's important to stress that no one of the positions is inherently better than the others. But you may well find that you have a preference for one or two. (Some positions, however, *are* more suited to deal with particular situations. For instance, many counseling techniques involve helping victims recovering from trauma to use Position 3 to review what happened. From there they are able to see that they did everything they could to deal with the situation as well as they could. They can then give themselves "permission" to move on from the experience.) As with so many tools in this book, you need to be prepared to be flexible and to use all three positions in a single interaction, if necessary, to help identify or solve a particular challenge—see "Cho Changes Position" later in this chapter.

You should find it relatively easy to spot the preferred position someone has in a specific situation. For example, you're talking to different donors after an event, going over how it went from their points of view. You ask each one, "How was the gala fundraising dinner?"

- One says, "I loved it. From the minute I walked in I felt part of something really special. The decor was amazing—all the glitter and ice-themed flower arrangements. As soon as I heard the music I was up on my feet dancing with my partner." (Position 1)

- Another says, "Initially there seemed to be a lot going on and I didn't seen able to get into the swing of it. I think I must have looked a bit naive walking in and staring round at the decor. But then when the music started my partner realized that I wanted to dance." (Position 2)

- And yet another says, "Everyone seemed to be having a good time when I arrived—it was clearly a fun event. I overheard a number of guests mentioning the decor. And the music obviously had people excited from what I could see from the bar. Eventually I ended up in the middle of the dance floor dancing with my partner." (Position 3)

If you notice their preference in an informal conversation it will help you to frame subsequent fundraising discussions with these individual donors more effectively.

Understanding perceptual positions can also be useful in *coaching* situations.

Cho Changes Position

Some time ago we had a colleague, Cho, who worked for us. She started being late for work three or four times a week, gradually extending to five mornings in a row. We needed Cho to change her behavior.

I took her into my office and sat her down. "Cho, don't you feel bad about coming into work late every day?" I expected her be embarrassed and hoped she would be contrite. Instead she was apparently merely puzzled and said "No." Clearly approaching the challenge through Position 1 wasn't going to have the desired effect. So I changed tack.

"Cho, how do you think I feel when I get into work early with a full schedule, and then have to spend time answering the phone for you and making excuses for you being late?" Again I'd hoped for embarrassment or even some sense of my concern. But again there was genuine puzzlement. Cho didn't do Position 2 either on this occasion.

I had one final try. "Cho, imagine Suzie [a close friend and respected colleague] was listening to us having this conversation. What would she say?" There was a pause—a sudden dawning realization. "Well," said Cho, "she might say that it wasn't fair that you have to take my calls." She then agreed to change her behavior.

Having tried the other positions, I had to get Cho into Position 3—the objective observer—to get her to understand the challenge. She simply didn't seem to be comfortable in Position 1, thinking about her own behavior, or Position 2, understanding my concern. As an influencer, that's why you need to be prepared to move a person round all three positions if necessary.

Deciding When to Use Each Position

A skilled influencer uses each of the positions appropriately and keeps them in balance. To maintain that balance, you need to be clear when to use each one. Here are some examples.

Position 1

- Being assertive and making sure your opinion will be heard—for example, before you go to a potentially difficult meeting rehearsing how you might answer the particular concerns of different board members.

- Setting an outcome. Position 1 is a very good frame of mind from which to answer the question, "What do I want in this situation?" (See Chapter Five, "Shaping Outcomes.") For example, when you're negotiating with an important businessperson and want to ensure you don't concede too many benefits in return for their sponsorship.

Position 2

- Reassuring the other person that you understand their situation—for example, a donor who's nervous about the size of a gift. This empathy will often gain you credibility with them.

- Trying to understand why someone is behaving in a way that seems against their interests. You might use this with a colleague who's behaving "oddly."
- Assessing the impact on the other person of the decision you're about to make. This is useful when you have to make a tough choice between your interests and those of someone else.

Position 3

- Dealing with polarized situations in which you need a balanced overview—for example, after an especially tense board meeting when harsh things were said and you need to get back on an even keel.
- Rehearsing what you plan to do or say and imagining how other people might receive it—trying to assess how the audience of multiple stakeholders might respond to your pitch.
- Reviewing a situation you think you handled badly. For instance, how you might have better managed a solicitation that seemed to go off track—the donor appearing quite negative and you speaking irritably. Is that really what happened? Or not? And if yes, what could you have done differently?

Choosing the Best "Positions" for Fundraising

As fundraisers it might seem obvious that we most often want to encourage donors to adopt Position 2—the perspective of the charity's beneficiaries—so that they can appreciate how important their donation is to the people directly affected. Position 2 has advantages, but it isn't necessarily *best*.

Let's work through a fictional case study. WaterforLife is a nonprofit organization. It works with people in rural Africa digging wells and running sanitation projects. By doing this it helps protect health. It also removes from young people in a community the burden of walking several miles each day to fetch and carry safe water. The WaterforLife fundraiser needs to convince a donor of the importance of a new local pump project. She might start by trying a Position 1 perspective.

"We know you're already a generous donor. Thank you so much for your support. I'm here today to ask you to consider contributing to our village water pump program. This will help almost six thousand children living in Northern Uganda—among them ten-year-old Hilda, a little girl the same age as your own daughter, Joanne. I'd like you to think back to when you were ten and compare your day with Hilda's. Hilda gets up at 5:30 A.M. to walk four miles along a dusty track to the nearest pump in the next village. There she fills two three-gallon jerry cans—like the ones I have here with me—to provide clean and safe water for her mother and four little brothers and sisters. She makes the same journey in the afternoon. My guess is that when you were ten you, like me, were woken by your mother way after 5:30 to shake you out of bed and tell you breakfast was ready. I guess too that the heaviest weight you had to carry each day was your school bag, and the longest distance was to and from the school bus. Hilda, on the other hand, carries large jerry cans a total of sixteen miles each day.

"We're worried that Hilda, and many other children like her, are missing out on the start and sometimes the end of school to make time to help out in this way. And we also think they're missing out on the chance to play as you and I did—and all children should."

Alternatively the fundraiser could frame the proposal in Position 2.

"Thank you for meeting me and for your generous support in the past. I know you've seen the report from our field staff telling you how much your help and support has meant to them. Now they've asked me to ask you to help with the village water pump project. Let me tell you who this will help. I'd like you to imagine you are Hilda, living in small village in Northern Uganda. You are ten years old. Every morning before school you rise at 5:30 to help your mother and younger brothers and sisters by walking four miles along a dusty track to the nearest pump in the next village. There you fill two three-gallon jerry cans with water. You balance one on your head and carry the other. Stopping frequently to change hands, you walk the four miles back to your house. You do the same in the evening after school. You'd love to have time to play—but you're always too tired.

"How do you imagine Hilda feels about spending up to four hours each day collecting water? How do you imagine her life might change if she just had the chance to attend school properly?"

Using Position 2, the fundraiser is asking the donor to experience what it's like to *be* Hilda—to empathize with her world. Once there, the donor might be much better placed to give—and to give generously. Our experience suggests if you have a donor who can move into Position 2 you'll find it a very powerful place from which to make a fundraising solicitation. So it's almost always worth trying a Position 2 perspective to see if the donor connects with it. To help with this make sure you also match the donor's preferred visual, auditory, or kinaesthetic modality.

Interestingly, some donors prefer to commit from Position 3. Let's assume the WaterforLife fundraiser is meeting a different donor. Our fundraiser knows that the donor struggles to "walk in another person's shoes," and his own comfortable lifestyle is worlds away from Hilda's experience. So our intrepid fundraiser takes an alternative approach.

"Thank you very much for your help and support in the past. I want to share a case study with you and to find out if you could see yourself supporting it. The case is about Hilda and six thousand other children like her in Northern Uganda. This is a picture of Hilda, her mother, and four younger brothers and sisters in their small village in Northern Uganda [shows photograph]. Every day before dawn her mother has to wake her and ask her to make an eight-mile round trip to collect water for the family, carrying two heavy jerry cans. She has to make the same trip at the end of the day. In the case study, which I'll leave with you, Hilda explains that this makes it hard for her to get to school on time and sometimes means she has to leave early to fetch the water before it gets dark. Her teacher is concerned of course but recognizes that Hilda has to help her mother. You can see how Hilda, her mother, and the teacher are all stuck and unable to make progress. If there were a pump in the village, Hilda would get to school on time, and would even have time for play with other children after school—something that everyone accepts is important for rounded child development.

"We'd like you to consider helping Hilda and the thousands of children like her. Imagine seeing yourself giving her the gift of childhood. Imagine being able to tell her she doesn't have to get up to fetch the water—and then listening to the family chatter when she eats breakfast with her mother and brothers and sisters. And how do you imagine Hilda's life would improve if she could join her teacher and classmates for the whole of the school day?"

The fundraiser is asking the donor to step into Position 3 to look at the very different world of Hilda, her mother, her brothers and sisters, and her teacher from the outside in. Implicit in this view is a comparison with his own, much more comfortable circumstances. Once the donor is in this position he might be better placed to understand—and like the donor in Position 2, to give generously.

As you read these little scenarios you might well find yourself thinking one is obviously "better" than the others. Actually they're not. They're all just different. But you probably have a preference for the one that matches your own approach.

Lighten Up, Spock

Some people find the idea of Position 3 intensely attractive. They see it as being an objective, rational, balanced way to explore things. And it's true, there are situations in which Position 3 is attractive *and* useful:

- *If you've been in a very stressful or distressing situation.* You can use Position 3 to help distance yourself from your over-strong emotions or response. Let's say you felt really let down or depressed after a particularly grueling meeting. Going into Position 3 for an objective review might help you realize it wasn't as bad as you thought.

- *To analyze what else you might have done.* Try replaying the situation as if it were a movie with yourself as one of the characters. Freeze the action at key points and think about how you might have directed yourself to behave or do something differently. (The role of "movie director" is a very useful one to use when thinking about Position 3 generally.)

- *Where you've received some challenging feedback.* Your chair has fed back negatively on how your recent report to the board was received. You're not sure if it's fair or balanced. So it's feedback, but how useful is it to you? You replay the events through your own perception, then through the chair's perception. And finally you replay through the position of, perhaps, someone whose opinion you admire and respect. You hear the third person give their verdict as if they were a judge on *American Idol*.

- *To assess things "live."* Let's say you're running a meeting. Parts of it are going well and parts badly. When you notice things are going well you decide to become a "Webcam" on the ceiling, and notice what's happening. And to do the same when things are going less well. From your observations you come to understand that closed questions stop the flow of the meeting and asking open questions moves it on. So you focus on using open questions.

While it's true the distance and balance provided by Position 3 can be very useful in a range of situations, it also has limitations. A purely objective approach will cut out too much valuable information.

Think of the occasions when Mr. Spock from *Star Trek*, or his latter-day incarnation, Data, were puzzled by the actions of humans. Feelings like love, loyalty, envy, generosity, and passion didn't make any kind of logical sense. The various captains—Kirk, Picard, Janeway, and so on—were better leaders *precisely* because they were able to combine the objective with the emotional. Emotions are very important in human transactions, especially philanthropy.

Position 4—Getting the Big Picture

There is a fourth position, developed in 1988 by a consultant named Robert Dilts (Figure 9.4). He called it the *meta-mirror*. We prefer to call it the "big picture" perspective. The purpose of the big picture is to help you get a wider perspective on a whole situation. Note that *wider* is different from *objective*. What we're doing here is to take other factors from *outside* the immediate situation into account—it's the bird's-eye or helicopter view.

Normally the three perspectives or positions will tell you

- How *you* feel or think about or experience something
- How *someone else*—the donor or beneficiary—feels or thinks about or experiences something
- How the *interests of these specific protagonists* are balanced or matched

But sometimes it's important to look beyond the interests of the direct protagonists—for example, to other stakeholders.

Figure 9.4

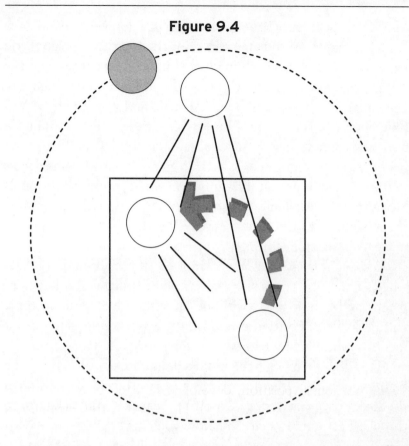

Some examples of when Position 4 is useful are

- Analyzing the impact of a profound decision that
  will affect a wide range of different stakeholders
- Deciding what to do in a difficult ethical situation
  or when values or principles are in conflict
- Moving outside a short-term perspective to think
  about the long-term outcomes or ramifications

We have found the big picture approach most useful in
deciding whether to launch a big campaign or go ahead with
a risky project. Here's an example. We were working with a

university in Peru. The director of development wanted to launch a major donor campaign even though there is very little experience of significant individual philanthropy in that country.

He thought about how this stressful, high-value, high-risk campaign would affect him and his wife and young baby. (And how good a success would be for his career.) (Position 1) He also considered how a successful campaign would help the beneficiaries—young people keen to gain scholarships and access to the new facilities that the campaign would pay for. (Position 2) He next tried to balance the strain on him and his family against the advantage to the beneficiaries. (Position 3) But he couldn't make a choice in Position 1, 2, or 3 on whether to proceed.

Position 4 then encouraged him to step back and consider whether the university was really ready to run such a big campaign, and run it well, without an established philanthropic culture in Peru. Position 4 told him it was too risky. He recommended running a more modest campaign.

This does take practice, and it's helpful to start by trying the big picture with a friend acting as a coach to guide you through the process of each step. In our experience you need to go through Positions 1, 2, and 3 before you try 4.

Big Picture Exercise

Choose a difficult situation involving another person that you'd like to explore and learn from. Then place four chairs to denote the four perceptual positions. Spread the chairs out so that you have to take several steps from one to the other. That way you can physically change perspectives as you move between them.

1. Sit at Position 1. Remember, this is *your* point of view. Look over at Position 2 and imagine the other person is sitting there. Ask yourself, "As I look at this person, what am I thinking, feeling, experiencing?"

2. Move from Position 1 to sit at Position 2—the *other person's* point of view. As you walk, consciously change perspectives. From here, imagine you are the other person looking back at yourself sitting in Position 1. Ask yourself, "As I look at this person, what am I thinking, feeling, experiencing?"

3. Move from Position 2 to sit at Position 3—the *independent observer*. As you walk, again consciously change perspectives. From this position, look at both yourself and the other person. What do you think about yourself when you look from the outside? How does your response to the situation and the other person's response look from here?

4. Now move to the last chair, Position 4—the *big picture*. As you walk, consciously change perspective. From Position 4, look at the situation and put it into the bigger picture of the overall outcome you're trying to achieve. In this context, is the challenge you're having with the other person worth the effort needed to solve it? Or is this one person the key to your resolving the situation? Also look back at yourself in Position 1 and compare your response there with that at Position 3. Then swap them around. For instance, if you felt anxious in Position 1 and sympathetic in Position 3, be sympathetic in Position 1 and anxious in Position 3. Does that change your thinking?

5. Still in Position 4, revisit the other person in Position 2. Are things different here now that you have reflected from the other perspectives? Have they changed?

6. Finally, get up and move back to Position 1. As you walk, consciously change perspective. Back in Position 1, from which you have to decide what to do, how are things different?

Using All Four Perceptual Positions to Reach an Answer

In the late 1990s a good friend of ours, Anne, worked as director of development for a large cultural institution in London. With her fundraising board she was running a £100 million capital campaign.

The campaign attracted an extremely generous benefactor who was prepared to personally donate £15 million. She "simply loved" the institution and the project, and declared that this was "just what I've been looking for." In return for her gift, she wanted a place on the board, and this was agreed.

Unfortunately, the dream donor rapidly became Anne's worst nightmare. She rang us in some distress. "The chair of the board and three key members of the team are threatening to resign. The donor is spending huge amounts of time here, "lording" it over the staff and telling them that it's her money that's keeping them in a job. And yesterday she reduced my deputy to tears. How on earth can I sort this out without losing her goodwill and money and still hang on to the team and chair?

Anne came to see us the next day. We got some more detail. As a result we decided to rehearse the first two perceptual positions with her. Anne sat in a chair labeled "Position 1." In Position 1 we asked her to tell us what she was thinking, feeling, and experiencing when she looked across to a second—Position 2 —chair where the donor would be sitting. "Anxious, angry at how many people she's upsetting, at a loss about what I can say that will help her understand that this situation has to change."

We then asked Anne to identify what she really wanted to say and do. We were getting her to a place in Position 1 where she could be assertive with a donor who could be more than a little intimidating.

Next we asked Anne to get up, give herself a small shake to get out of Position 1, and walk over to the chair at Position 2 to get into the donor's point of view. What was the donor thinking, feeling, and experiencing as she looked over to where Anne would be sitting in Position 1? "Hmmm. Unappreciated. I've given these people a large sum of money—the biggest of anyone—and yet I don't seem to get any special treatment. I'm a successful businesswoman and want to help, and I'm pretty sure I know how to, so why don't they just listen?"

Putting herself in the donor's shoes gave Anne a real insight into the donor's experience of the world. She knew the donor wanted more appreciation and acknowledgment.

With our help, Anne developed some ideas to deal effectively with the donor, and she left feeling confident that she could have a constructive meeting. She rang to say it had all gone according to plan. The chair and the team members had agreed to stay on. Success!

Not for long. Just two weeks later, Anne called again. "I've just had the most appalling row with the donor. I tried doing what you taught me again—my view then her view—before I went into the meeting, but it didn't work this time. What am I doing wrong?

Anne came back to our office and—still using chairs to signify perceptual positions—we "replayed" the disastrous meeting. This time we added a third chair and asked Anne to let go of the first two positions and look at the exchange from an independent point of view—Position 3. What did the exchange look like from the outside? "A battle of wills between the donor on the one hand and the board, the team, and other donors on the other—with me trying to mediate. The trouble is, I can't seem to hide my impatience from the donor, and she's reacting against it. Also she *says* she likes feedback but she doesn't really."

We worked some more with Anne, teasing out possible approaches for speaking to all the key protagonists. Position 3 had allowed Anne to access a more objective perspective.

A month passed with no word from Anne. Then we got a call. "You're going to hear about it on the grapevine soon so you might as well know now. Our chair has resigned. The donor has just lost us a £5 million gift through sheer rudeness to another donor. I'm thinking about leaving myself."

We persuaded Anne not to resign just yet. She loved her work, had been enjoying the campaign, and was devoted to the institution. She came to see us.

Anne felt that the situation was probably irredeemable. It was time to introduce her to Position 4—the big picture. Instead of examining just herself and the donor, as she had done in Position 3, we asked her to look at the impact on everyone else involved in the campaign—the board, the team, and other new and potential donors. How were they being affected by the donor's behavior? Anne spent some time listing a whole host of adverse impacts. We let her talk, with some prompts to encourage her to be as specific as she could. Then we asked her the questions she herself had been skirting around for some time, "Is this donor worth it? Do the negative effects now outweigh the benefits of her gift? If you returned the money, would you be in a better position to complete the campaign successfully?" After a short pause, Anne answered the questions simply, "No, and yes, and absolutely yes." She went back to the institution to meet the donor.

Position 4 gave Anne a bird's-eye view of the problem. The big picture enabled her to see the full impact of the donor's behavior including its effect on the likely success of the campaign.

A footnote before we end this story. The donor did leave. And that move unblocked a logjam, and the campaign went from strength to strength as a more positive culture developed.

Summary

Perceptual positions are an essential part of the effective influencer's toolbox. You can practice them in a range of situations—from coaching sessions with colleagues to sponsorship negotiations. If you think of yourself as a movie director creating the influence movie you want, you can write the script and then establish how it might appear to the different characters—including yourself.

There are three main positions from which you can experience any situation:

- *Position 1:* using your own direct experience and ensuring you are in touch with your own feelings and concerns
- *Position 2:* from the perception of the other person, using their experience and concerns to understand how they feel—and how you appear to them
- *Position 3:* in the objective position of an observer, being able to review the interactions between you and the other party—balancing concerns and feelings

Each position has significant advantages and disadvantages depending on the situation. All can be effective in fundraising.

Many people have a preference for one or two of these positions in terms of how they record and retrieve experiences. You can establish that preference by asking the donor to recall a situation they've been in when others were present. By matching their preference, or at least by understanding it, you can create fundraising stories or proposals that will be more attractive to the donor or influence target.

A skillful influencer will be able to move flexibly between the different perspectives to build rapport with others in "live" situations. This perception adds an extra or deeper layer of richness to the rapport when you also match the appropriate visual, auditory, and kinaesthetic modality.

This skilled influencer will also be able to review or revisit past situations they have been in and use the different positions to work out

- What went well and why—in order to reproduce it
- What went less well and why—to avoid repeating a similar mistake

This playing back of the movie can create a powerful and effective learning approach.

There's a fourth position that is useful when you're trying to see the much wider context for a situation. Position 4 can be thought of as the helicopter or bird's-eye view. You should use it when you feel concerned that you may need to locate any situation in a wider social, ethical, or strategic context.

Part Five

Persistence

10

HELPING DONORS SAY "YES"

The final cog in our influence process is *Persistence*. Even if you plan every element of your message perfectly, it won't always work the first time. So the successful influential fundraiser keeps trying—adapting tactics and approaches until they achieve their will-formed outcome. Both this chapter and Chapter Eleven will help you make your persistence focused.

The way people express ideas gives us important clues to how they filter information to form judgments. If we understand and respond appropriately to these clues we can help donors and others to say "Yes" more easily. Specifically we look at

- How individuals sometimes use one of three unhelpful processes to form their views
- What we can do to identify and tactfully challenge these inappropriate or unhelpful processes
- How, by asking better questions, we can help donors to clarify what *they* really think, and gain insights into how to change their perspectives

More Than Language

People prefer different language systems for communication—visual, auditory, or kinaesthetic. If you switch *your* language to the preference of the person you're speaking to, it can make it easier to get your message across and build rapport. But although matching language styles will always help improve communication, it's not enough to guarantee that your ideas will be accepted.

Sometimes it's necessary to go deeper into the influence process and consider how the donor actually *filters* information and ideas. Once you understand the processes she uses to do this, you'll be able to present your ideas to her in a way that will make them more acceptable—and you can help the donor to say "Yes" more frequently.

Loose Talk—Loose Thinking

People sometimes use language quite loosely. Using loose or imprecise language can make it hard for them to say—yes and may even lead them to say no.

Look quickly at the three rectangles pictured here.

Now look away.

It's clear what they say isn't it? Really? What they *actually* say is

"Once in a *a* lifetime"

"Paris in the *the* spring"

"A bird in the *the* hand"

We guess that many of you read the text as only having one "a" or "the" in each sentence. In that case you were reading carelessly.

Now try this. Read the following sentence and then count how many Fs there are in it:

FINISHED FILES ARE THE FINAL RESULT OF YEARS OF SCIENTIFIC RESEARCH COMBINED WITH THE EXPERTISE OF YEARS.

The answer is seven. You probably got fewer.

Exercises like these demonstrate that we often miss nuances in language, or draw inaccurate conclusions about situations, or even change information in our heads in line with assumptions we already have. We are all, sadly, a bit loose or imprecise with the way we take in and review information. So when donors prioritize information, think about what's important to them, form their opinions, and make decisions, they will *also* often miss data, make assumptions, and change reality in their heads.

Three Unhelpful Opinion-Forming Filters

Donors, and the rest of us, make changes to the way things are in reality in specific patterns. This isn't a random process. These patterns can be thought of as *opinion-forming filters*—or, more accurately, *opinion-distorting filters*. By noticing these filters at work we can present ideas or information in a way that helps donors to say "Yes."

There are three main opinion-distorting filters that you will notice people using when they talk and express their opinions or ideas. These filters are called *deletion*, *distortion*, and *generalization*.

We explore what these filters are and how each of them works. We also help you recognize them, and suggest what you can do to counter them if they're getting in the way of your influence efforts.

Deletion

Deletion is when someone pays attention to some elements of his or her experience and ignores or removes others.

We all practice deletion. For example, how often have you bought a new car—let's say a Volvo—and then begun to notice that there are lots of Volvos on the road? The other Volvos were always there. All that happened was you *used* to delete your awareness of them. And now you don't.

Our brains do this to stop them from going into overload. The same phenomenon means we don't listen to every little sound around us in a room, or take in every detail of decor. If we did we'd find it very hard to get anything done.

But this natural process can have more challenging implications. For example, people who support a particular political party will often ignore evidence of their party's "bad" behaviors, preferring instead to select the actions and activities they perceive fit with their positive opinion. It's hard, when you press these people, to get a rational answer about *why* they choose not to notice these contradictory behaviors.

For fundraisers, *deletion* can be a challenge when donors don't see the failings of another cause they support, or they only focus on its positive points as a way to turn down your request for funds. Or they may "delete" your successes to concentrate on some negative publicity you had in the past.

Table 10.1 Deletion. (The donor misses useful or important information and reaches an inappropriate conclusion.)

The kinds of phrases you might hear when deletion is happening. (The donor has erased some essential bit of data or a particular context hasn't been acknowledged.)	"I gather from the way you answered my phone call that your charity isn't so good about social inclusion and diversity principles." "I only give to causes that share my Christian values—but you're not a Christian organization, so how can you share my values?" "I was surprised that the board chair doesn't understand my nervousness about overhead costs."
The types of questions to ask to clarify what's being deleted. (Ask questions that clarify what's actually being said and get more information about what's being missed out.)	"In what ways are we not good at providing services for or including disabled people?" "What are the values that you see as basically Christian—and how don't we match them?" "Can you tell me what made you concerned about overhead costs?"
How to deal with it.	Get more information to help you establish what information is missing for the other person. You then need to help them put it back in.

The Deleting Donor

A Canadian charity was raising money for work with the victims of domestic violence. The head of development met with a donor who seemed happy to support the Refuge Programme, which provided safe houses for women who had left their partners. But the donor then went on to say the gift was on the condition that none of her money was used to support women who had *stayed* for any length of time with their abusive partners because "By staying, they're deliberately putting themselves in danger. That's just stupid."

At this point the development director reckoned the donor had deleted from her understanding the impact abuse has in undermining a woman's confidence. The resulting low self-esteem might make her unable to consider life outside the relationship, no matter how terrible the situation. For that donor, however, anyone who didn't just leave was simply being "stupid."

The development director couldn't accept the gift on these terms. She had to think quickly. "Could there be any other reason aside from stupidity why a woman wouldn't immediately leave an abusive partner? What if children are involved?" That good question gave the donor food for thought. She began to think maybe domestic violence victims who stayed weren't necessarily doing so out of stupidity.

Getting Past Negative Deletion

Once you've recognized that a donor is using negative deletion, you can try to put back the missing information or ask questions to help *them* put it back. This helps to move them onto a more positive position—one from which they may agree to your ask.

The easiest and most effective way of challenging a deletion that's working against you is by asking questions to help the donor "fill in" the missing bits of information.

Table 10.1, on page 184, shows how to recognize and deal with deletion.

Distortion

Distortion is when someone consciously or unconsciously creates a meaning or interpretation about something that might not be true, on the basis of a limited amount of experience. Often this involves linking several unconnected events or experiences. Again, we all do it.

Here are some examples of distortion:

- You learn that a key donor has complained about you and go out to lunch to try to calm down. When you return you see two colleagues in the office whom you don't get on with very well laughing and whispering. You imagine they're talking about you and that the donor's complaint is all around the office.

- A major donor is angry that his name wasn't recognized by the receptionist when he called to ask for a copy of the annual report. "The whole place is going to the dogs!" he says. "You've abandoned the stewardship approach."

Getting Past Negative Distortion

Once you've recognized that a donor is using negative distortion, you can try to undo the misinformation and move them on to a more positive perspective. The most straightforward way to do this is probably by showing that the two experiences the donor has connected aren't really linked at all.

So with the donor whose name wasn't recognized, you need to start by apologizing for the receptionist's failure. Then ask if there could be explanations other than the organization's stewardship going to the dogs. You might suggest the possibility the receptionist could have been under a lot of pressure at that time, as she was handling both reception and the switchboard. Or perhaps a poor headset made it difficult for her to hear clearly.

This tactic doesn't always work, but if you can succeed in helping undo the negative distortion, your donor is in a better position to say yes to your proposition.

Table 10.2 shows how to recognize and deal with distortion.

Table 10.2 Distortion. (The donor draws a false or inappropriate meaning by linking two unlinked issues or experiences.)

The kinds of phrases you might hear when distortion is happening. (Clues here are that there are two bits of experience being linked that are not connected.)	"If you're careless and can't spell my name accurately on the DM packages you send me, you're probably just as careless with my money." "The fact that you don't attend church on Sunday means you're not really a Christian—and I only support Christian causes." "I have to say I find your approach patronizing. That whole presentation with the silly clip art was designed to talk down to us."
The types of questions to ask to clarify what's being distorted. (Ask questions that uncover how the individual has come to a conclusion—what's their evidence?)	(Having apologized for the misspelling!) "Is there anything in our impact report that suggests to you we aren't efficient?" "Are there any circumstances in which a person could be Christian and not attend church?" "What specifically in the presentation did you find patronizing? Was it just the clip art or the content?"
How to deal with it.	Ask questions that enable you to establish exactly what the conclusion is and what the evidence is for it. Especially try and decouple the two irrelevant factors that have been linked.

Generalization

Generalization is when people consciously or subconsciously create a "universal" truth from one or two limited examples. In generalizations, we tend to develop rules and principles, which is why you often get a clue when you hear words such as *all*, *every*, *constantly*, and *always*.

A simple personal example might involve a friend with an unhappy romantic life who says, "All men are rats. I should just accept I will never be happy." Is that strictly true?

Here are some other examples of generalization:

- We worked with a fundraiser who said, "I'm hopeless at social events—I always put my foot in it with
  donors I don't know." In fact this had only happened once, but her tendency to generalize meant
  she saw all the successful events as exceptions.

- A warm prospect apparently on the verge of making
  a substantial gift to a homelessness charity has backed
  away. The chief executive goes to see him. The donor
  explains, "This article in the *New York Times* concerns
  me. It's clear all charities are spending too much money
  on administration. And administration is not what I want
  to fund."

Getting Past Negative Generalization

Once you've recognized that a donor is using negative generalization, you can try to establish the limits of their perspective
and move them on to a more positive position. As with deletion
and distortion, it doesn't always work—but if it does, it will help
your donor to say yes.

Table 10.3 shows how to recognize and deal with generalization.

Table 10.3 Generalization (The donor takes a small number of examples and makes an inappropriate larger rule or principle.)

The kinds of phrases you might hear when generalization is happening. (Listen closely for words such as *never*, *always*, *continually*, *constantly*, *only*, *all*, and *every*.)	"Charities always send out too much wasteful junk mail." "Only Christian charities can be trusted to do a job properly!" "Fundraisers are never really interested in you—they always want to get their hands on your money." "Board meetings in this organization never start on time."
The types of questions to ask to clarify what's being generalized. (Ask questions that help shift the individual's frame away from the generalization.)	"Are there any people who like to get information from charities in the mail?" "Are there any non-Christian charities that do good work?" "Are all fundraisers like this or just some aggressive ones?" "Have we ever started a meeting on time?"
How to deal with it.	Try to help the person understand the limitations of what they're saying—that it constrains them, their thinking, and their ability to support you.

Multiple Filters in Action

It's possible to hear all three filters in the same conversation. For example, a fundraiser approaches a donor to ask for a major gift. The donor *actually* says, "I guess that you and the team have worked hard putting together this proposal.

I really appreciate the time and effort you've put in. And I have the resources I'd like to contribute to a project in this field. But I can't commit to a donation in the foreseeable future. The basic challenge is I'm not convinced about the quality of the program you're asking me to support. If the independent evaluation had been more positive I could have done something. But the answer can't be 'yes' as things stand."

The nonplussed fundraiser goes back to the director and reports the conversation like this, "Well he was very positive generally and especially about the proposal. I think he's a great prospect. He said he had the money lined up for a project like this. We just need to convince him a little more on the effectiveness of the program."

In this case the fundraiser is using the filters to conceal lazy thinking. What we have here is the following:

- ☐ A *generalization:* The fundraiser said "he was very positive" when really the donor just said thanks for the effort.

- ☐ A *deletion:* The donor talked about *"the basic challenge . . ."* which the fundraiser ignored in her report back to the director.

- ☐ A *distortion:* The last thing the donor said was *"the answer can't be 'yes' as things stand,"* and the fundraiser translated this into "the donor just needs a bit more convincing about the program's effectiveness."

Beware Positive Filters

There will be times when you notice these filters at work and you're tempted to leave them in place because they complement your cause and sit with your own point of view.

- "After talking to that homeless person at the shelter and her good experience of the services you provide I'm sure you're the very best homelessness charity in the city." (Positive generalization!)

- "Okay, so the student results haven't been great for the last four to five years, but the vision—a college that helps disadvantaged adolescents achieve excellent results—is still exciting and relevant." (Positive deletion!)

- "That moving production of *La Traviata* explains why sharing opera as widely as possible is the most important cause in this city." (Positive distortion!)

You might be tempted not to question positive filters that benefit your organization. (Why rock the boat?) Be careful though. Sometimes it's better to try to help the person have a more *realistic* view of your work. If you're on a pedestal, the only direction is down. So when you come across inaccurate positive filters, you might want to try to restore a more realistic perspective by using questions similar to those we've outlined for redressing negative filters. You need your donor to have a *balanced* view—otherwise they might be disappointed at some future point when you can't live up to their super-high expectation.

Mental Decision-Making Software—Metaprograms

There are some even more specific ways in which people tend to understand and transmit their experiences. These pieces of mental software are called *metaprograms*. Put simply, metaprograms are more specific preferences or habits in thinking.

Again, the way people speak gives an excellent insight into which of these programs they are using to make a decision or process an experience. But unlike the deletion, distortion, and generalization filters, these preferences are not about loose thinking. Metaprograms are more refined or specific ways to think.

Being skilled in identifying and using metaprograms is very useful when you want to

- Frame a case statement or proposition in ways that appeal very specifically to a particular individual
- Discover why someone isn't responding as you thought they would to your proposition

About twenty-five different metaprograms have been identified by psychologists and consultants working in the field of NLP. Each metaprogram offers insights into different ways of thinking. However, there are probably just five that are really useful to fundraisers:

- Match or mismatch
- Associated or disassociated
- Toward or away from
- Big chunk or small chunk
- Past, present, future

In each case your preference may differ from or be the same as the person you're communicating with. It's important you don't *assume* anything, but build your approach on observed behaviors. That way you are much more likely to succeed in influencing them.

Match or Mismatch

Have a look at the image pictured in Figure 10.1. Take a minute to think about it and then describe the relationship of the objects.

How did you describe that relationship?

Figure 10.1

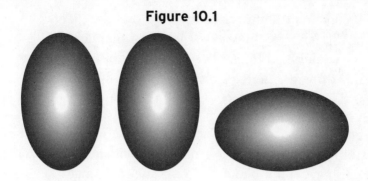

- "There are three ovals, all apparently are the same size, and one is over on its side."
- "There's an oval on its side and then two others upright. They might be the same size."
- "There are two upright ovals, and then one upright oval that's fallen over on its side out of the set."
- "There are three objects—one on its side over to the right, one next to it in the middle upright, and then another one further away from it also upright."

Notice that at least one of these descriptions seems like the most obvious one to you. And one or two of them are descriptions you would never have dreamed of saying—they seem just too "odd." That's because some people initially sort for *difference* (mismatch) and some people sort for *sameness* (match). Oh, and some people sort first for *sameness* and *then* for *difference*.

Let's try another example. Take a look around at the room you're in. If you're in your office, compare it to your favorite room at home. If you're at home, compare it to your office. When you make the comparison, do you

- Predominantly think about things that are the same? (It's also very simply furnished—like home it's got photos of my family, and it's a mess like the lounge.)

- Predominantly think about things that are different? (Here is so hi-tech—I love the simplicity of my uncluttered home, I've got photos of my family at home—here it's charts and graphs, the office is tidy thank goodness—unlike the lounge.)

So how can the fact that some people look for similarities and others for differences—*match* or *mismatch*—be useful in fundraising? Think about the response you might get to your fundraising proposal. "Thank you for explaining your case about your work on international development. But I wonder how you're really *different* from CARE? I need to see some extra value to make it worth my while contributing." A question such as this is a clue that this *mismatcher* needs some *difference data* before they will say yes. Equally, a question such as, "This is all very interesting. But I'm keen to support a range of causes committed to international development. How do you *complement* CARE?" is a clue to a *matching* preference. In that case look for *similarities* to share.

Obviously it's better to know your prospect's preference before you begin the "business" part of the discussion. So it's worth having some standard cueing questions or situations to elicit or establish their preference. For example, try asking

- How they like this location compared to where you met last time.—"It's about the same distance from home." (match) "It's a much more businesslike venue for the board." (mismatch)
- How lunch compared to last time.—"They have the same kind of menu—a mix of salads and more substantial dishes." (match) "The service was much slower and less friendly." (mismatch)

Associated or Disassociated

A second very common and useful metaprogram is "associated or disassociated." (This metaprogram relates very strongly to the work in Chapter Nine, "Understanding Their Point of View.")

To help make the distinction, recall a genuine conversation you had recently that was difficult or distressing. Take the time to recall it in as much detail as you can. Notice how you communicate the experience to yourself. What comes first, the challenging image, the harsh words that were said, the feelings of anger and frustration?

Now notice how you *accessed* the memory. As it came to you, did you shut your eyes or defocus and replay the situation as if through your own eyes and ears? Or did you keep your eyes open and recall the event as an external observer, hearing yourself speak, seeing yourself in that situation?

Here the distinction is between

- *Associated:* in your own body through your own perception
- *Disassociated:* observing or noticing yourself from outside your own body

Some people associate very easily. They can recall situations from their childhood incredibly strongly and can "flash back" to the feelings, the sights, the sounds, and even the smells from their early life as if they were there now. Some of them do this so strongly they can even "associate" as other people. So when you say, "Imagine you're a ten-year-old girl in northern Uganda obliged to walk six miles twice a day for water. It's only 7 A.M. but you feel tired in the heat because although you've already walked four miles, you still have as far to go again," you'll have some of your audience visibly wilting as they step into the body of the girl—or what they imagine that girl to be—and experience the walk.

Others will find it hard to "be" the girl in any way. They find it hard to associate. So for them you say, "Imagine you're watching a television documentary about the challenges of growing up in a rural community in the developing world. It tells you about a young girl—maybe just ten years old—and it shows her walking to collect water from the well in the next village. What do you feel as you watch the little girl on the TV screen? If you were there, wouldn't you want to help her carry the heavy jerry cans, or say something to encourage her?" For these people the preference is to respond through disassociation.

Noticing this distinction can be important. Our experience suggests that many fundraisers find it easy to associate, but not all donors. This can explain why some donors don't identify emotionally with the cause in the intense way you do. If you're aware your donor prefers to be disassociated, you need to reframe the proposition to meet his or her needs.

Toward or Away From

Think about a personal goal you have—maybe to do with your weight or fitness, or with a flagging relationship.

Notice that you thought first either about

- A *positive* situation you wanted to get into—to look great on the beach or to have a really happy holiday

   or

- A *negative* situation you wanted get out of—to lose weight, to stop having rows and feeling stressed

These two approaches represent two different kinds of thinking—moving *toward* and *away from*. As with the other metaprograms, we need to be prepared to adapt our fundraising communication to reflect the donor's preference. The classic use for this metaprogram when communicating to donors is to present our proposal in terms of moving *toward a solution* or *away from a bad situation*. For example:

- "Your donation to our hospice will ensure cancer sufferers can avoid the pain and indignity of unprofessional care at home or impersonal care in the hospital." (away from)

   or

- "Your donation will help us create a positive and holis-
  tic haven where we can support the cancer patients
  as they move toward a peaceful death." (toward)

Different donors are likely to have a preference for one
way of shaping the proposal over the other. Notice that *you'll*
probably prefer one of the preceding statements over the other.

Again, you can use questions early on—in the telephone
call to arrange the solicitation meeting—to cue yourself about
which of these preferences is most evident in the prospect. If you
know they've just had some change in their life—new job, new
house, that kind of thing—find a way of asking them why they
chose that change. They'll most likely respond in a *toward* or
away from style: "I wanted to get away from that neighborhood"
or "I wanted to come somewhere warmer like here." Once you
know their preference you're in a better position to frame your
ask in the way that's most effective for that person.

Big Chunk or Small Chunk

People process ideas at different levels. A key way to help
connect and change a person's ideas and beliefs when trying to
influence is to do what's called "chunking up" and "chunking
down." Essentially this is the same as "zooming in" and "zooming
out" or, if you like, "big picture" and "small picture," with
graduated steps in between.

To illustrate how chunking works, think of an airplane:

- To *chunk up* even more, think of categories such as "kinds
  of transport." To chunk it up more, think of "travel."

- To *chunk down*, think of "speedy planes." To chunk it
  down further, think of specific planes like a Boeing 747 or a
  MiG jet.

Big chunk or small chunk is a very useful metaprogram to help you get on your donors' wavelengths and to help resolve disagreements.

For donors who prefer *big chunk*, you might have a proposition that tells them something like the following:

- "The situation for people with HIV/AIDS in sub-Saharan Africa is terrible. As a society we need to address this issue."

A slightly *smaller chunk* might be

- "In Zimbabwe there is simply not enough medical aid available for the fifteen million people with HIV/AIDS. As residents of a developed and wealthy country we have a duty to help them."

A small chunk would be

- "Abotho is a town in Northern Zimbabwe where almost fifty thousand people are HIV positive. That's a population the size of our community here in Smallville. We need to connect to that community and support them."

And an even smaller chunk would be

- "In Abotho I met Lasha, who was infected with HIV by her husband. She now has full-blown AIDS. Lasha can't look after her children, aged five and seven, without access to medication. But medication costs $25 a month. Lasha—when she can work—earns just $250 in a *year*. Your gift of $1,000 will not only pay for the life-saving treatment she needs for the foreseeable future, it will also buy her the food that will help to keep her healthy, and it will pay for her children's education. They, at least, will have a better start in life."

Notice that small chunk doesn't mean a small or individualized gift. You could finish up the last ask with: "And if you can gift $10,000, we can bulk-buy the medication and you could help twenty women like Lasha to have a future."

Chunking up is very useful when you're trying to find common ground, and chunking down when you want to get to a specific deal. Going either way is relatively easy to do with practice and good questions.

To *chunk up*, try these questions:

- What will this give us or you?
- What purpose will be served by doing that?
- What's your intention by that specific request or action?
- What general principles or values can we agree on?
- What general situation or cluster is this an example of?

To *chunk down*, try these questions:

- With what specific results?
- What are examples of this concern or advantage?
- What specifically is the challenge or agreement?
- What would be a preference between one or more possibilities?
- Give me some detail or an example of this.

Past, Present, Future

This is one of the easier metaprograms to use in fundraising influence. Again, if you're curious and take the time to observe, you'll find that people tend to

- Talk about the past a lot

  or

- Focus on the present

or

- Anticipate the future

You might experience all of the above from one person, but the key issue is, Which is really important to them at that point?

Think back to when you were a child on a long car journey. Or notice the behavior of your own children if you're a parent. What's your *default* question—or the question your children ask?

- "How long have we been traveling for?" (past)

  or

- "Where are we now?" (present)

  or

- "How long till we get there?" (future)

Chances are you—or they—asked the same question over and over again. You or your children may just be being annoying. Or your past, present, future orientation may genuinely be revealed in this question.

Let's put this in a fundraising context with three potential donors to an art gallery:

Donor A says, "I've been very keen to help you with the art gallery—it's the kind of project that fits well with what I've wanted to do for ages as a social payback. But I've been at this place with cultural projects before—lots of good ideas and only a partly formed initiative. So I really need to see the solid foundation you can build on." This is a person who's very committed to the *past* as a source of sorting information.

Donor B says, "I'm very keen to help you with the art gallery. I'm excited about your plans for the opening and it fits with where I am just now with my giving. But I'm not sure that I can really grasp all the ideas and concepts in the air at the moment. Where are we really starting from? What's the status of the project as of today?" This is a person who's very committed to the *present* as a source of sorting information.

Donor C says, "I'm very keen to get started and help you with the art gallery—and I'm excited about your forward-thinking ideas for the opening. It could possibly fit in with my investment plans. But lots of this seems quite risky—and a number of the good ideas are still being formed. So I really need to see where this is going." This is a person who's very committed to the *future* as a source of sorting information.

To frame your ask around *the past:*

- Stress your track record
- Look for examples of similar challenges and similar successes
- Emphasize the length of relationship you have or their track record of commitment

To frame your ask around *the present:*

- Establish the current challenge
- Outline the need for action now
- Develop why there is a window of opportunity

To frame your ask around *the future:*

- Create an energizing vision
- Stress the potential for results and momentum
- Emphasize the likely negative consequences if action isn't taken

What's Best?

There's no best or worst, or right or wrong metaprogram. All have value in different situations and with different donors. And we all have access to all of them to some extent. The secrets are

- Learn to understand your own preferences in the way you frame beliefs and interpret data
- Learn to adapt your language and the way you transmit ideas to meet others' preferences

See also Appendix C, "Translating Your Case," for a detailed worked example of how to use some of this mental software to frame fundraising proposals.

Here are some final points about the nature of metaprograms. There are two sides to every filter, but they aren't an *either-or*. And they aren't *fixed*, although we all have preferences. They exist on a spectrum, and just where a person is on a particular spectrum can vary depending on the situation.

Summary

The basic NLP modalities—visual, auditory, and kinaesthetic—are primarily about communication styles. When we match them we're matching the way people talk. It's like going to Mexico and deciding to try to speak Spanish so you can be better understood.

Donors and others are sometimes unclear in the way they process information or experiences. This can lead them to misrepresent the evidence of their experience. It can also mean that they say "No" based on a false way of thinking. The three basic unclear thinking filters are

- Deletion—removing information
- Distortion—linking information or experience inappropriately
- Generalization—forming an overarching view when there is no general principle

If you hear a "No" to your proposal, ask questions to help clarify where it's coming from. And if you can't understand why someone is turning you down, try to spot where their thinking is out of kilter.

At a more refined level you can establish what specific bits of mental software people are using to process experience. These bits of software are called metaprograms. They are a very fine level of filter that you can use to shape proposals for individual donors.

There are five metaprograms that we find important in fundraising:

- Match or mismatch
- Associated or disassociated
- Toward or away from
- Big chunk or small chunk
- Past, present, future

If you key into your donors' preferences, you not only understand their thought processes better, you also have an invaluable insight into how best to present them with a proposal.

11

DEALING WITH OBJECTIONS

We can't always get it right. Even with the best preparation things go wrong in a solicitation meeting or at a presentation. But a key element of success in influence is *Persistence*. Persistence is a powerful mix of resilience and flexibility—not simply stubbornness. So as fundraisers we have to learn how to recover and adjust our approach when the donor presents an unexpected challenge.

Specifically, this chapter explores how to deal with objections. It offers solutions for three types of difficult situations you might encounter:

- How to deal with "No." There are actually nine different No's in fundraising. This is good news because it means an initial negative from a donor doesn't necessarily mean "No" permanently—it's often simply an invitation to ask a better and more focused question.

- What to do with feared but reasonable *killer questions*. These questions expose a real weakness you have or a potential flaw in your work that might emerge if you don't take effective action. Rule number one is don't bury your head in the sand and hope these questions are not asked, but anticipate and plan your responses.

- How to respond to specific *patterns of decision making* in donors and others. We all—including donors—have four basic approaches to or strategies for making decisions. If you understand the donor's preference for one or more of these strategies you can help them make a decision in your favor. You will also understand why people sometimes change their minds.

The Nine Fundraising No's

People won't always agree with your fundraising proposal. Even when you use the most sophisticated influence approaches, the reality is that you are still likely to get a "No" more often than a "Yes." The difference between a successful and an unsuccessful influencer is that the former doesn't necessarily accept the first "No" as a definitive answer. The successful influencer responds by being curious about what exactly the donor means.

There's Darwinian logic to this, at least in fundraising. Put simply, if you only asked people who would definitely say "Yes," or if you only asked for the size of donation that you were sure they would definitely give, you'd

- Be working off a very, very small sample of potential donors
- Probably tend to "under ask" by framing your proposition very low

And the negative payoff is that you'd possibly

- Be letting down your cause and the people you're there to help

So to be successful as a fundraiser you need to learn to deal with the possibility of rejection. And in particular you need to deal with *initial* rejection and be able to analyze it more closely. That first "No" may not be as bleak as it appears.

To help you manage and interpret the possible rejections you might experience we've created a "No" typology. In our experience there are essentially nine fundraising No's that prospects use. With the first eight of these, if you follow up with a better question you may well get a better result. Only one of these responses—the last one—genuinely means "No, go away." And if you hear this No, you should leave. But mind you still say "Thank you" to the prospect for his or her time—see the section "Be Polite" for the possible payoff for good manners.

The nine fundraising No's are

1. No, not for this
2. No, not you
3. No, not me
4. No, not unless
5. No, not in this way
6. No, not now
7. No, too much
8. No, too little
9. No, go away

Each of these No's has an underlying reason or explanation, which a skilled influencer will seek to uncover. And that's why dealing with "No" properly requires that you ask a different or better question rather than simply giving up.

Be Polite—Good Manners *Do* Pay Off in Fundraising

There's still a place for good manners—thank goodness—in fundraising. Suzanne Rolt is director of the prestigious St. George's Concert Hall in Bristol, United Kingdom. Part of her job is to bring the people of Bristol an extraordinary range of musical experiences. To do this she needs to program challenging contemporary music alongside the more established classical canon. Not surprisingly, she relies heavily on money from trusts and foundations to support the work.

Suzanne came along to a seminar of ours about a powerful approach we have developed for structuring foundation proposals. She went away to try our methodology, and she was successful with nearly all her proposals. But two foundations said "No," as they'd allocated all their money for that year.

Undeterred, Suzanne decided to try a little old-fashioned courtesy. She wrote back to the two foundations, saying thank you to them for taking the time to consider her proposal. And as a mark of gratitude for their investment of time, she offered them two free tickets for any of the trustees or foundation staff who would care to attend a performance at the venue.

Both foundations responded almost straight away. Their replies revealed something we as fundraisers should find damning and embarrassing. Both said no one *ever* wrote back to say thank you for taking the time to consider a proposal *when they'd rejected it*. Applicants wrote and complained about the unfairness of the process, wrote extra data to try to change trustees' minds, and inquired about the next occasion they might resubmit. In all the years the two foundations had been giving away funds, no one had simply written to thank them for *their* efforts.

Indeed, they were so impressed by Suzanne's politeness that they both offered small *ex gratia* grants to St. George's—even though their initial response had been to reject her application.

Suzanne now writes and says thanks to *everyone* who rejects her proposals. In her mind it's about a relationship. And she accepts that relationships can get off to a poor start. But she reckons, and so do we, that any relationship worth having is worth working at.

Getting from No to Yes

Table 11.1 explores our "Nine Fundraising No's" typology. In it we suggest why you might get a particular "No," what the donor might *really* want from you, and how you could respond in a way that might lead to a more positive outcome.

Table 11.1 Nine Fundraising No's

No	Reason the Donor Gives	What the Donor Really Thinks—and How You Might Respond
No, not for this	"You've asked me to support your education program for children, and I'm not interested in work with children."	"Why don't you ask me to support your work with adults or elders? I'm interested in that kind of work." *If they are in some way drawn to your work, what might they specifically be interested in?*
No, not you	"I'm not comfortable with you soliciting this gift." (The solicitor is maybe a thirty-year-old woman and the donor a man of seventy-plus.)	"I'm seventy years old and want to talk to someone my own age who shares similar life experiences and understands how I feel about the importance of a legacy gift." (Or "I want to talk to someone of my faith, or with my sexuality.") *Who's the right person to ask the donor, whom they will feel comfortable with?*
No, not me	"I'm not the right person to ask—I can't or don't make those decisions."	"I don't make these decisions. You should talk to my partner—she decides about our charitable giving." (Or "You should talk to the marketing director" if it's a company, or "one of the other trustees who has an interest in this field," if it's a foundation.) *Who is the key decision maker who will decide whether to back this proposal?*

(continued)

Table 11.1 (continued)

No	Reason the Donor Gives	What the Donor Really Thinks—and How You Might Respond
No, not unless	"You don't seem to be offering me what I need or want in return for my gift."	"I need to have my deceased partner's name on this building as part of the gift fulfillment." (Or "No, unless you provide the following commercial benefits" if it's a sponsorship.) *What is it they really want, and can you ethically or reasonably provide it?*
No, not in this way	"You've asked me for cash and I can't help with that."	"I could help with some other kind of support through my business interests, such as vehicles, printing, and back-office services, but you don't seem interested in other kinds of support." *If not money, how else can they help?*
No, not now	"I can't help you at this time."	"Why don't you ask me for a donation in a year's time after my daughter has graduated from university?" (Or "When I've sold the company" or "Toward the end of our foundation's financial year when we know the resources we have left.") *When would be a good time to make this ask?*
No, too much	"I can't give you that amount of money."	"I don't have that sum available or it doesn't fit with my commitment to your cause. Ask me for a different—lesser—sum that will be meaningful for you *and* is within my range." *What sum might be appropriate and acceptable, and still help with your project?*

Table 11.1 (continued)

No	Reason the Donor Gives	What the Donor Really Thinks—and How You Might Respond
No, too little	"I want to do something bigger and more important, and that sum doesn't relate to that feeling or commitment."	"Ask me for a different—larger—sum that will be meaningful for me and relates to my ability to give. I want to make what I perceive as really a significant difference or an impact." *What kind of sum is appropriate, and can you use it properly?*
No, go away	"No"	"I've thought about your proposition and decided that it isn't what I want to support." Say thanks and back away. (Though try the Suzanne Rolt politeness tactic—it might just work.) *Is the door closed, or what might have to change for there to be a possibility to reestablish the relationship?*

In truth there are probably more than nine No's, but these are a good start in that they force you to listen carefully and actively to the response—"No" needn't be final.

It's especially important to try to work out which No is being used:

- When you're in a live one-to-one situation in which the initial rejection might seem to be the end of the conversation. It helps you look beyond your own immediate disappointed reaction.

- When you're helping a colleague who's returned from an unsuccessful prospect visit and they need help to identify what else they might have done to recover a situation that was going wrong.

No and Chunking Up

The tactics we outlined in the preceding section are good behavioral responses to the "No." But there is a link to another element in the book that reveals some of the hidden or deeper processes behind a "No" that can become a "Yes."

The specific questions you ask to distinguish different No's link strongly to the "chunking up" technique we discussed in Chapter Nine, "Understanding Their Point of View." That is, when you reach a block or challenge you can scale an idea or concept "up"—make it bigger—to find out where there *is* agreement. So when someone says "No" to your ask, you might *chunk up* with "Well I'm disappointed you can't support our education program, but I'm guessing from what you said earlier you *do* feel the general principle of outreach work is a good one?" If the answer is "Yes" to this, then you've successfully chunked up and simply need to find an alternative outreach program for the donor. If the answer is still "No" when you chunk up to outreach, you may want to consider asking a more general chunk-up question, "What was it that first attracted you to our cause?" Such a question might elicit an answer—"Well, I really became involved because of my late husband's admiration for your CEO"—that takes you off in a completely different direction. And at that point you "chunk down" to find out what the donor's late husband was interested in.

The important thing about the nine No's is that you can generally plan for them and prepare an appropriate response or have a better—different—question ready.

Anticipate the Killer Question

A second essential aspect of dealing with objections lies in anticipating the killer question—and preparing an answer for it. The feared but reasonable killer question is the one you have been dreading. It's the flaw in your case you know exists. Or, it's the challenge about your organization's work you hoped had been glossed over. And you pray the person you're trying to win over won't ask it. But what if they do? You *have* to have a response.

Killer questions can take a range of forms:

Scandal: Every organization has its scandal—or scandals. (If you don't know about the one(s) that your organization has it's because you've not been paying attention or haven't been there long enough.) Sometimes that scandal can almost bring the organization down, as in the Covenant House example later in this chapter. Sometimes it can be a minor failing that was blown up by local press. Are you aware of any organizational skeletons—either current or in the past? Do you know all the facts? How was or is this issue being dealt with? How will you respond to a challenge about it?

Crisis management: Even if you don't have a scandal at the moment or in the recent past, is there a potential one that might emerge—a problem that could expand into a crisis without proper advance contingency planning? It could be financial, or to do with waste, or to do with abuse. Again, have you prepared an answer or a strategy to deal with this?

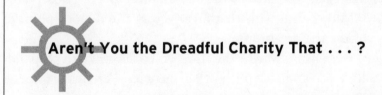

Aren't You the Dreadful Charity That . . . ?

Judy Beard, our much respected colleague at =mc and former fundraising director at one of the United Kingdom's leading cancer charities, tells the painful story of being woken up at midnight by a call from Ecuador with the news that a supporter was missing and presumed drowned at the start of a sponsored trek designed to raise money for the cause. The death (it was only confirmed three days later), it's important to stress, was a dreadful accident and not the charity's fault.

With her events manager, Judy broke open the emergency contingency plan created by a former employee. It consisted of two sides of paper, and she'd reached the end of the recommended actions by 3:00 A.M. All the rest she had to make up as she went along, including working out how to break the news to the poor supporter's parents. ("Hi, your daughter was trying to raise money for us . . . and died in the attempt," is a difficult influence situation, we guess you'd agree.) The organization had a plan to *stop* things going wrong. But if they *did* go wrong—as, sadly, things do—it didn't have a plan to deal with the fallout effectively. As soon as the crisis was over, Judy made sure there was a detailed plan and proper procedures to deal with anything approaching a similar crisis in the future.

As a fundraiser you may have to live with the consequences of something going wrong in the organization. When a donor raises this issue you have to have a response. It's not acceptable to say, "I don't deal with that area." From the donor's point of view you *are* the organization.

Poor benchmark: Maybe the thing you'd most like to keep hidden is how you compare with other agencies. Perhaps you spend more on administration than other comparable organizations, or maybe your service or artistic record is poor compared to your main rivals. How will you deal with it if the donor is aware of this? One way is to put a better spin on the figure or comparison that's being used. ("It's true we're more expensive, but the quality of our work is better.") Another way is to acknowledge that you don't compare so well and to adopt the Avis "we try harder" approach. You might actually gain some credibility by the admission and could, if you played it right, win an advantage.

Developing Organizational Influence—The Covenant House Case

You may well be familiar with the story of Covenant House, the charity set up by Fr. Bruce Ritter in 1968. Within ten years "Father Bruce," as he came to be known, achieved considerable media fame as he and his colleagues focused on rescuing homeless and disadvantaged teenagers. Volunteers and donors flocked to help, inspired especially by a series of regular monthly newsletters that Father Bruce penned. (These newsletters themselves are marvelous examples of influence through simple, powerful communication.)

By 1990 Covenant House's success was seemingly unstoppable. Annual turnover was almost $100 million, and there were programs nationwide. Ninety percent of the funds came from individuals, especially wealthy Catholics. Throughout this period the charismatic Ritter remained in charge, attracting universal praise for his passion and communication skills.

Then a young male prostitute claimed Father Bruce had paid him for sexual favors. Other accusations emerged, including ones of financial impropriety. Within a few months, Ritter was forced to resign. Covenant House was soon struggling to survive as donations fell by $25 million in twelve months and public confidence disappeared. People associated the organization so strongly with Ritter that his personal failure was seen as an organizational failure.

The board began to develop strategies to rebuild the organization's reputation with donors. These influence strategies included

☐ The board of directors carefully and painfully examining its own role in governance and oversight, undertaking a challenging audit of their own culpability in the scandals

☐ After a careful search, appointing Sr. Mary Rose McGeady as the new leader, an experienced CEO with a background in running child-focused services

☐ The new CEO, working with senior board members, preparing briefings for donors and supporters on what was happening at key stages in the process, and seeking their advice

☐ Researching and then introducing a number of sophisticated protocols on child and young person protection, which became a model for other organizations to adopt

☐ Being as open as possible through careful media briefings about what had happened and what had gone wrong

Almost twenty years later, Covenant House is still not the organization it was. But it has reestablished a measure of credibility by the action it took, and the methodical way it moved from dependency on a charismatic leader and developed its *organizational* influence.

Helping Donors Decide—The Secret Is Timing

An important but neglected aspect of fundraising influence is the issue of *time* in donor decision making. If the potential donor puzzles you by not saying "Yes" when you expect them to, then you need to consider reviewing what their *convincer strategy* is.

Convincer strategies are the distinctive approaches individuals have to using *time* in making decisions that they feel comfortable with and committed to. You will certainly have a convincer strategy of your own—and may feel puzzled about why others don't *decide* in the way you do. Being able to recognize different convincer strategies is useful in fundraising influence—in particular, they should help you understand why a donor sometimes seems to say "Yes" and then changes her or his mind.

There are essentially four time-based approaches to decision making:

- Automatic
- Number of times
- Period of time
- Consistent over time

Remember these approaches are about the *different* ways people like to make decisions. So they relate to the question, "How often do you need to be convinced to feel secure?" In this section we explain how to recognize each strategy in a donor and then offer suggestions about how you as an influencer should respond.

Before we go into these in detail, you might like to see if you can work out your own convincer strategy. Here's a simple experiment. Think about how you might buy something like a stylish jacket or a pair of hi-tech trainers—that is, an item that is not cheap, but not life-threateningly expensive either. So thinking about trainers. Do you see a pair in the shop and decide there and then to have them? Or do you see a pair, go and look for something similar elsewhere to compare price and value, and then return to the shop? Or do you decide you like them, but consciously go away and have a cup of coffee to reflect on whether you're being silly and if you really need them? Or do you buy them—but then spend ages on the way home looking in the box and seeking reassurance from your friend who's with you that they were a good buy?

On reflection, you'll probably find that you have a preference for one of these approaches. Note, as with many of the approaches or psychological frameworks we covered in the book, this is a *preference*—not a fixed mind-set.

Let's describe each approach or strategy and consider the implications for influence in a fundraising setting.

Automatic

People with the *automatic* decision-making response form quick and often almost instant judgments. They will develop a basic like—or dislike—for whatever it is they're being asked to decide about almost immediately. This could obviously apply to donations but might also apply, for example, to hiring people, or friendships, or investment decisions. Note that individuals with this preference don't necessarily say "Yes" to something straight away. But they make a gut "Yes" decision early on. They may then carry on listening and gathering information that supports their initial gut reaction.

As part of this basic approach to decision making, they will often assume that the person talking to them is competent and has the knowledge and ability needed to do their job. So you should be able to convince this person of your proposal quite easily. But the problem is, so can everyone else. . . .

The basic challenge here is twofold:

- They will make a decision on not enough data, meaning that their commitment can unravel.
- The last person they see will have a strong and probably deciding influence.

A donor with an *automatic* preference is likely to readily accept your case and support you if you are organized and persuasive. You will get lots of positive feedback as you share your ideas. But the deal is not yet done. The secret here is to make a convincing and powerful case and then get a *formal commitment* as soon as possible. You should also try to ensure that such a donor *really* understands the case rather than just agrees with it on a superficial level.

Following are some typical challenges:

- If you're not in touch for a while this kind of donor some-times gets caught up in another organization's cause. Don't treat this as disloyalty—it's just the way they think.

- If they have a close adviser, partner, or colleague who tries to dissuade them from their early commitment, that individual may indeed be swayed. So it's very important that you find out whose opinion they value, and work to include that person or those people in your influence activity.

The secrets of success when you have a donor with an automatic preference are

1. Make sure that they are given all the information they need and that you have answered questions they might hear from others when you're not there.

2. If you get them to commit early then acknowledge and record this commitment formally—ideally in writing.

3. Ensure that you continue to maintain contact with the donor and go back to check that the commitment still holds.

Number of Times

A person with a preference for this strategy will need to see, hear, or go through any proposition you make *a number of times* before they are convinced. Typically this person will compare a range of products before they buy, visit the same product a number of times, or talk their decision through several times with the salesperson. Essentially they need specific reassurance on issues as they occur and will internally question any decision they make.

If you are "selling" an idea or seeking a gift from someone like this, be prepared either to roll out the idea X number of times, or offer them X number of alternatives that meet their concerns, or present the idea in X number of ways. How many the "X" represents depends on the number of times the person needs to receive and process your proposition in order to be convinced—it could be three, five, or any number.

Donors with a *number of times* preference will need repeated reinforcement of the message. They may ask you how you compare to another cause in terms of efficiency and effectiveness. They may also ask to meet you again—and at that meeting you may well go over the same ground as previously. With this type of donor you need to be patient and remember that there is probably a *pattern* to the number of times they need to be convinced.

Here are some typical challenges:

- They want to be given a range of projects they could support and then to be allowed to choose between them so that it's *their* choice.

- They may want to visit a specific project or meet a senior program officer several times to be reassured their money is going to be "invested" well.

Donors with this preference take up a lot of time, and sometimes you can lose patience with them because you can't understand why they don't just make a final, *committed* decision. However, it's worth persevering if they're *genuinely* potential major donors.

Period of Time

As the name implies, individuals that have this approach to deciding want a *gap* between the ask and their decision. They need to think through any decision over a *period of time* to feel comfortable—it may be a few hours or even months. (It was probably someone with this style who invented the idea of the "trial period" for goods and services.) These individuals hate feeling pressured and may ask for time to reflect before offering a response of any sort.

Donors with the *period of time* approach need "space" to process your case or proposition. They don't like to be hustled or pushed. They probably want you to agree to a fixed time by when they will give you their decision. This should be quite formal. They will normally then stick by their decision. (This formality and desire to commit to a date is what distinguishes them from time wasters.)

Some typical challenges might be the following:

- You need a decision in a shorter timeframe than they feel comfortable with. If you really can't postpone the decision, try to identify what the key motivator or "hot button" is. (See Chapter Three, "Understanding Donor Motivations.") Or, ask for an "in principle" yes that then leaves an opening for them to change their decision later if they feel unhappy.

- You may find their overall timetable too long for the major gift you are seeking. Try "chunking" your ask. (See Chapter Ten, "Helping Donors Say 'Yes,'" on big chunk or little chunk.) This way you might see if packaging the gift or commitment in smaller chunks reduces the time they need to reflect.

So if the donor says they will think about it, ask them how long they need. And allow them to have that period. If you chase them too soon, or offer them too many different choices, they'll feel harassed. Keep within their comfort zone and you're likely to get better results.

Consistent Over Time

This type of person needs *repeated demonstration* over time to make a decision. And they are never *really* 100 percent convinced that they've made a good choice. Each time you try to convince them, you need to re-prove your case. When they go out to buy a new DVD recorder, they will look at many models before making a decision. And even when they've bought one, they will seek other options, looking for flaws in their existing purchase.

As a fundraiser making the ask, you have to work hard. Unlike the automatic decision maker, these people consider that you're only as good as your last piece of work—they won't give anyone the benefit of the doubt.

Donors who need repeated demonstrations are never completely happy. Every time they renew their membership or annual gift they need reassurance. They may *seem* satisfied and then come up with a new concern, which you're expected to address. Your overall approach here involves lots of patience, and making sure that you have uncovered *all* their concerns through careful questions.

It's probably a good idea to have a regular cycle of communication with these people anyway. Notice that they may have a strong need for reassurance in terms of what we have earlier called "hygiene factors." (Again, see Chapter Three, "Understanding Donor Motivation.")

Here are some typical challenges and the responses you should offer:

- They keep raising a new objection, and that prevents them from committing. Try to find someone they respect and admire and use that person's influence to have an impact. You might even use the influencer to help tackle the objections overall. Above all, make sure you give these donors *reassurance* on an ongoing basis.

- You may find that the donor's objections are quite abstract and they seem slightly disconnected. Try to get the donor to "associate" with the cause using the techniques we explored in Chapter Nine, "Understanding Their Point of View." You may want to help them to identify a beneficiary—a child who has to walk eight miles for water, an elderly woman who needs care, a minority student who needs support to make it through college. Use this beneficiary as a touchstone for their decision.

As buyers of ideas, these prospects need constant confirmation and reassurance about the wisdom of their decision. It's important to acknowledge that you'll never *completely* win them over to your point of view. "I know I can't personally absolutely convince you that this is the right project for you to get involved in. You'll only know when you see the way beneficiaries gain and grow from your support."

People with this decision-making preference are very high maintenance and require very hard work. But they will also ask you very good and searching questions about your proposition, which you should be able to answer. If you can satisfy them, you can satisfy anyone.

Welcome to the Dragon's Den

There's a great Japanese TV show called *Dragon's Den*. It has versions in the United States, the United Kingdom, and Canada. If you haven't seen it, it's a cross between *American Idol* and *The Apprentice*, in which a panel of judges—all successful entrepreneurs turned venture capitalists—meet a parade of would-be entrepreneurs seeking investment and advice for their companies, products, or services.

Each neophyte entrepreneur gets two minutes to make his or her pitch to the panel, hoping to convince them to invest money and time in their project. The show is by turns inspiring and excruciating. Many of the best ideas fail because of the way they are presented—with the contestants concentrating on themselves and their proposition rather than the judges and their needs and interests.

If the putative entrepreneurs *did* spend some time observing the judges at work on the show, they'd discover that a major factor in the way the judges decide is their different convincer preferences. In the U.K. version, two judges choose using the *automatic* strategy. They take an early shine to an idea—or dismiss it—within minutes. If they like the applicant and their idea then she or he can only lose the support of these two judges by doing something very stupid. But if the judges' opening remarks are negative it's not worth the applicant trying to win them over, as their initial *antipathy* will not be argued away—whatever the proposition.

Another judge uses the *period of time* strategy. He asks questions throughout the process, forming a judgment as he goes. He listens intently to the views of the other judges, and his face shows his internal weighing up of issues. He does all this without committing until the end of the process, when the deal, in terms of the show's rules, is that he needs to make a decision.

The last two judges use the *number of times* strategy, relentlessly asking quite pointed questions on a few key issues in different ways. Their aim is to establish *exactly* what the proposition is and its business potential. They will often appear to be satisfied by an entrepreneur's answer and then return to a topic, such as their cash flow projections, demanding some new assurance. You can see applicants really wilting under this minutely targeted questioning.

Interestingly, none of the judges is *consistent over time*—which is likely what makes them successful entrepreneurs. Such people would presumably find it difficult to achieve success with a *consistent over time* approach to business. They would make a decision and then be so nervous about it that they might unravel the whole deal.

Discovering a Donor's Decision-Making Strategy

How do you find out someone's convincer strategy preference? Well, as before, we recommend subtly asking them to provide you with the information you need. As with many of the techniques in this book, if you talk to a person in a careful and structured way you can discover a lot about him or her. You then simply need to pay careful attention to their responses for insights into their decision-making approach or preferences.

For example, having built rapport at your meeting, try asking a donor whose preference you're trying to establish about a recent big purchase they've made, such as a car or a house. The donor might give a range of responses that will help you. Let's take the car: "I usually let my wife decide all that stuff, but she and I just fell in love with our new car when we saw the color." (automatic) Or, "We liked the new car, but I always think it's important to sleep on a decision like that. So we went back next day just to check we still felt the same." (period of time)

Obviously, don't form a judgment on just one piece of information. Be sure to check out your thinking in several contexts—holidays, recruitment, previous gifts to charities. Once you're confident about the strategy, you can then work with the approach that the prospect most values and is likely to be most responsive to in terms of actually committing to the gift.

Finally, take a moment to think back to the earlier questions about your own trainer buying or other decision-making habits. What would you say *your* dominant approach is? Does that affect how you view other people when they go about making choices in a way that's different from yours? Do you share a decision-making approach with your partner, or are you different? If the latter, how does that affect you when you're trying to decide on doing something together?

Summary

When you're fundraising you have to be able to deal with donor objections. These objections come in many forms. Some of them are very proper and serious and may challenge your whole approach to stewardship, or question the validity of the project. Some are simply to do with the *way* individuals want to be asked, or *who* they want to ask them, or *how* they make decisions. You have to be able to deal with all kinds of objections.

There are three common sets of objections that you will experience and should plan for to succeed in fundraising influence:

- The *Nine Fundraising No's*. The harsh and seemingly unforgiving word "No" can in fact be an invitation to ask a better and more detailed question of the prospective donor. The No's range from situations in which you have simply misjudged what is important to the person to situations for which you or they are the wrong person to be having the discussion. Only one No is a direct request to go away. Above all, if you do bump up against the No word, don't take it personally—use this challenge as a chance for you to grow and learn.

- The *killer questions*. Killer questions are those which expose a real challenge to your case or proposal. They will expose a current or potential weakness in your organization and are challenges you should have specific answers to. It's worth brainstorming about what would be your killer questions and, if they're likely to come up, sharing the answers widely across the organization. Above all, if your organization has mishandled donor money or relations in the past, be candid about it and explain how the organization has grown and what it's learned. How you handle killer questions will make a massive impact on your *long-term ability to fundraise generally*. Whatever you do, don't bury your head in the sand and ignore the possibility these will come up.

- The four *convincer strategies*. Everyone has different ways of finally making a decision, all of which relate to time. The good news is there are only four classic patterns. (You experience these very often in sales settings.) They are important at the point at which you're looking for a decision on a gift or gift commitment.

Try to establish your prospect's preference by finding out about how they make decisions generally. You can do this in the course of normal conversation about other everyday things they do, such as buying a refrigerator or clothes. The four classic patterns are

- *Automatic:* deciding straight away
- *Number of times:* comparing and contrasting
- *Period of time:* choosing a period for reflection
- *Consistent over time:* needing reassurance

You need to be prepared with a different response for each of the decision-making patterns.

12

CONCLUSION

As we indicated right at the start of the book, our approach to influence in fundraising is designed to help you achieve the results your organization needs in the fast-changing and more competitive fundraising environment that exists today.

We've combined a mixture of trial-and-error-based practical experience with a detailed study of best-practice thinking drawn from academic disciplines such as psychology and neurology. The result is the 5Ps Model of Influence.

We've worked to make the 5Ps as simple as we can. But, *simple* doesn't mean *simplistic*—so we've also worked hard to provide you with information and examples on the best and most powerful approaches we can offer. Simple also doesn't mean *easy*.

To summarize the 5Ps, they are

- *Passion:* the essential, emotionally intelligent drivers that have convinced you about this cause, and those that will motivate others

- *Proposal:* the key organizing frameworks and models you can use to shape and communicate your idea or cause—often called a case

- *Preparation:* how ready you are emotionally and intellectually to influence someone and deal with any challenges they might raise

- *Persuasion:* how skillfully and flexibly you use and adapt the powerful psychological and neurological techniques we've shared to communicate your cause

- *Persistence:* how ready you are to keep trying creatively and imaginatively to achieve the result you need—despite setbacks

Note that even when the 5Ps are together in sequence they don't make a straightforward step-by-step model. Life, and influence, and indeed people, are all too complex for that. But they do represent a checklist for you to consider as you work through any influence process. The challenge for you now is to use those skills, techniques, and approaches in your work.

Five Last Principles to Take You Forward

This book doesn't pretend to be the definitive last word on influence. So now that you've worked through the chapters, we have five last principles to guide you through your journey of *continued* learning. For each principle we've suggested how you can apply it to carry on developing your skills and abilities.

1. If you always do what you've always done you'll always get what you've always got.

This well-known aphorism actually contains quite a lot of wisdom that relates to influence.

Most important, as we've emphasized a number of times—probably too many for those of you with an *automatic* decision preference—the person who is most ready to change and adapt in any situation is likely to have the greatest influence. The practical implication is that you need to practice being flexible in *every* aspect of your communication approach—from the words you choose in your proposal to your blink rate with the prospect. So don't just apply the techniques that appeal to *you* from the book. Try them all.

However, let's quickly balance this plea for flexibility by reemphasizing that of course it's *essential* that you begin any influence effort with a specific and concrete outcome. It's true that you can never go into any situation absolutely sure you'll achieve your exact outcome, however. So you also have to be able to respond flexibly in *outcome* terms if the information about the situation or the donor changes. That's where the LIM-it technique is enormously useful.

Finally, don't just try to influence in fundraising situations. Begin by practicing at home or in the office. Try case-making and metaphors to get a raise at work, and rapport-matching in bars to meet new people. (One of our colleagues refused to be impressed by our influence skills until outstanding rapport at check-in secured her an upgrade to business class on British Airways. Now she's a fan.)

2. Everyone has their own unique map of the world—to change it you need first to understand it.

This second principle sits at the center of our thinking about effective communication and influence.

Each of us has our own unique mental "map" or "model" of the world that informs the opinions and beliefs we have. These maps are different ways of codifying and organizing the same mental-map data, and they provide us with a way of navigating in social and work situations. The perceptual positions, the language styles, the metaprograms, motivators, and hygiene factors—all are ways to help you understand a part of someone's map.

It is important to stress that none of these maps is absolutely "true" or "objective," especially not yours. No matter how skilled you are in influence, or how certain you are of the justness of your case, you can't simply introduce your own map and impose it on others. Indeed, initially, you have to *suspend* your own map of the world to be able to enter into someone else's. To be a successful influencer, you need to recognize, understand, and work with other people's maps.

There are some very practical implications for this. You have to accept that your definition of a major gift may not be the same as someone else's. (They may want to go bigger or smaller according to the Nine No's.) Or you may have to appreciate that the reason why someone agrees to make a gift may be very different from the reason that would make you do so.

So above all be genuinely *curious* about other people and their beliefs and opinions and how these relate to their behavior. Note the patterns they have and work to match these.

3. You already have most of the resources you need to influence people.

If that principle is true, you might want to ask, "Did I need to buy this book?" Our answer is, well, yes and no.

In the broadest sense we mean that so far in your life you've probably been able to deal with almost all the situations in which you have found yourself by drawing on *your own* inner resources or capabilities. As a child you somehow managed to learn complex body language things such as learning to walk, and acquired sophisticated linguistic skills like talking, without attending a personal development program or reading a book on it. You may well have managed to find a partner without studying the skills of rapport. So you are capable of achieving incredibly difficult things *naturally*.

We believe that many of the techniques and approaches in this book are likely to have made "sense" as you read about them. You probably even use some of them already—even if it's unconsciously. What we have aimed to do here is to raise your current competence to a *conscious* level so that you can learn to apply your skills *systematically*. We've also, we hope, introduced you to some new techniques.

We've given you a set of tools. Use them by all means. But also work to develop your own skills through observation and practice. If you learn to notice how things work you can then apply those lessons. Take time to watch people in the process of influencing others.

4. If someone else can do something, you can learn from that person's success—you just need to model their skill.

Notwithstanding what we've said in our third principle, there are always quicker ways to learn, and one of the best is to model other people who are already good at influence.

We've based much of our advice on the study of fundraisers and other nonprofit leaders who are outstanding influencers. You may remember some of the names—Valerie Humphrey, Giles Pegram, and Kate Gilmore. Sometimes we had to spend a long, long time studying them to try to identify *what exactly* helped them succeed.

Occasionally we've offered you the distillation of abilities taken from individuals *we* know and have observed influencing. But we're guessing you also know some high achievers too. Look out for those successful influencers in your life—professional and personal—and study how they get their results.

Practically, step one is to spend time and patience developing your *acuity—the ability to spot what exactly is happening in any situation.* You'll need this ability to discover what it is that other people actually do. (Often that feels like the body language version of active listening.) Next step is to identify the key belief or behavior they use to achieve the result they want. Then have a go yourself—and *voila*, you're modeling.

Finally, don't be afraid to cast your net wider and record politicians, religious leaders, or celebrities onto DVD to explore different approaches.

5. The meaning of your communication is the response you get—there are no failures in influence, only outcomes.

You cannot *not* communicate—even silence creates an impression or has an impact. And any kind of communication creates a response or feedback in the potential donor—whether as a listener or reader. The result is we can always get feedback, whether or not it's what we want or expect.

When something doesn't go as we planned we tend to see that as *failure*. Depending how mission-critical the situation is we might then get frustrated, angry, sad, depressed, worried, guilty, or whatever. None of these responses really serves any useful purpose.

But what happens if we see the unexpected and challenging response as *feedback* rather than *failure*? A real-life, real-time experiment in how not to do something? If we respond like this then, instead of getting angry or whatever, we've learned something. Instead of feeling "bad" we can now begin to create a new and better plan of action—and try again.

As with modeling, in order to learn to improve your influence you need acuity to identify the feedback you get in a given situation—from detailed written comments on the structure of the case you shared to a frosty stare in reply to your request for a donation. Once you've received the feedback you then need to establish what it *means*. This sounds easy but it's hard sometimes to take feedback objectively, especially when it seems very challenging. (The frosty stare, for example, might be someone's way of testing out your commitment, but it *feels* threatening.) When you're able to make an accurate assessment, one practical payoff is you'll have developed your emotional intelligence.

Is this just *Walton's*-style, rose-tinted-glasses, positive thinking? We think not. Thomas Edison, as you may know, tested 1,009 materials over two years which were *not* suitable as light bulb filaments before he found *one* which worked. J. K. Rowling's first *Harry Potter* book had to be published privately by her after eleven publishers rejected it as "unsellable."

Commitment to your cause should help you find the emotional fuel—the passion—to keep trying.

Join Us and Others in Learning

To help you keep learning—and to help us improve our own knowledge—we've love you to keep in touch. You can contact us through our company at www.mangementcentre.co.uk.

We have also created a special Website associated with this book to help you improve your influence abilities: www.theinfluentialfundraiser.com . On the Website you can get

- Extra downloads with more information on influence techniques
- News of seminars and training that you can attend
- Webcasts and podcasts you can download

And, finally, there's

- Space for you to give us feedback and share your own case studies of success

We look forward to hearing from you and keeping in touch.

Bernard Ross and Clare Segal

Appendix A

ACCESSING EYE CUES

It's important that you pay close attention to nonverbal clues when you're in a situation with a person you want to influence—for instance, when you're making the ask to a potential donor. These clues can give you essential information on how the ask is *really* going, whatever the donor is actually saying. Remember, many donors are too polite or nervous to tell you truthfully what they think or feel. Note also that in some cultures it may be rude to simply give a straight "No."

As we saw in Chapter Eight, the *words* a person uses provide an important source of information on which sensory system they prefer when thinking—auditory, visual, or kinaesthetic. There are, however, *other clues* to how someone is processing information. These clues are helpful if a donor is silent and you need to try to work out whether they're making a picture in their mind, or feeling something strongly, or replaying a conversation.

The Cell Phone Giveaway—Other Clues as to How People Are Thinking

Next time you're out and about, try moving up a grade from people-watching to people-on-cell-phones-watching—especially those who are too far away for you to hear the words. What are those people doing as they speak?

☐ Holding the phone in one hand and pressing it against the opposite ear so that the arm goes across their body, eyes tending to move horizontally from side to side? And possibly wrapping the other arm around themselves to make a cocoon? Leaning up against a wall or a tree, or whatever comes to hand, apparently processing carefully what the person at the other end is saying before responding? Speaking quite evenly and in a measured way? You can be pretty sure they have an *auditory preference*.

☐ Phone clamped firmly to the ear, looking up to the right or left and gesticulating as they talk? Probably walking—or even pacing around—as they talk? Talking fast and seeming to inter-rupt the person at the other end at times? The likelihood is they have a *visual preference*.

☐ Phone held to the ear but not so tightly, tending to look down and to their right? Touching things as they speak—running a finger over a smooth surface, feeling the softness of a piece of fabric in a clothing depart-ment? Playing with a pen? Speaking more slowly and with longer pauses between talking as they think? Chances are, they have a *kinaesthetic preference*.

The Secret's in the Eyes

The key nonverbal cue is eye movement—literally, where a person's eyes move when they're thinking.

Consider these situations:

- *Asking a friend if she had a good holiday:* She gazes off into the distance—almost defocusing—and says, "Yes, the sky was so blue, the water crystal clear . . ." and so on. She's obviously right back there and enjoying it.

- *Asking a colleague what he thinks he should do in a difficult situation:* The colleague looks up, looks down, looks to the left and then right. He then says, "I don't know."
- *Asking a donor "What's the key thing that persuaded you to join our cause?":* The donor tells a story slowly and in the telling spends a lot of time looking down at the floor. She appears to be quite emotional.

What we're noticing here is an interesting and useful extension of the verbal cues to thought processes we get when people are talking. Put simply, when we process information neurologically—in our brains—our eyes move in predictable patterns. These patterns can give us a clue as to the sensory system being used as the person thinks—whether it's visual, auditory, or kinaesthetic.

For example, when a person thinks about a visual representation of something that they can remember happened—such as what color sweater they wore yesterday—their eyes tend to move up and to their left. Equally, when you think about how sad you were when your grandmother died, or how mortified you were when you knocked a glass of wine over a potential donor, your eyes tend to move down and to the right as you process the sad or uncomfortable feeling you have.

So why is accessing eye cues important in a fundraiser's influence skill set? Because they allow you to gain an accurate insight into your donor's preferred way of processing information without any words being spoken by them.

For example, imagine you're making a presentation to a corporate board. You're pitching to the board of Tecfood Store to be their next Corporate Social Responsibility–funded charity. This is the first time you've met them, and you've no idea what their different sensory preferences might be. So in your presentation you make sure you bring in all three systems—asking the board to see, hear, and feel your proposition. (But not all at the same time!) You talk about the situation your users find themselves in before your charity gets to work with them—lonely, isolated, cut off from the world, no sense of self. Notice who looks down and to their right, and tick your mental checklist—you've spotted the members who are predominantly kinaesthetic.

Paint a picture of how their support will help your users, and notice who looks either straight ahead or up and to the left or right. Another tick on your mental checklist—you've spotted the members who are predominantly visual.

Thank them for hearing your proposition, and ask them to listen carefully to the benefits to the company. Look around and see whose eyes move horizontally to the left or right. One more tick on your mental checklist—you've spotted the members who are predominantly auditory.

You're giving this group of people exactly the same information, but they are each interpreting that information according to their sensory preference. By *consciously* using the language of all three preferences, you work to ensure that everyone has the opportunity to be fully engaged by your proposition. You also give yourself the opportunity to find out more about each individual—even though it's you that's doing the talking—so that you can use more of their preferred modality in future meetings, and build even stronger rapport.

Eye Movements and Their Meanings

As you'll see in Figure A.1, in all there are seven clearly defined eye movements. Note that these movements may be quite quick. The person you're speaking to may be making eye contact, then they will break eye contact briefly while they "process" in a particular way, and once done, will return to making eye contact. So you need the skill of *acuity* to be fully turned on and to spot what's happening.

Figure A.1 Seven Eye Movements

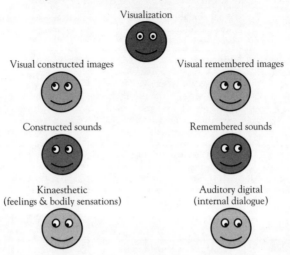

Interestingly, these movements seem to be common cross-culturally. At =mc we've studied this phenomenon in countries as diverse as Ethiopia, Sweden, Argentina, India, Thailand, Australia, and the United States. In every case the *basic* movements are the same. One caveat, however—the movements are sometimes reversed in right- and left-handed people.

Table A.1 explains each of these eye movements in greater detail. In the right-hand column we've taken the example of raising funds for a women's refuge and illustrated how you might use this awareness to modify or adapt your communication for the donor. You may want to reinforce a specific preference as you notice that the donor responds more strongly to one or more of the statements. In that case you use more of those.

Some Pointers to Help Develop Your Acuity

People can look in various directions for a range of reasons—they heard a sound, they have something in their eye. So don't make assumptions too quickly. Access eye cues in association with the words a person uses where possible. Or, raise the same issue using the same modality and see if you get the same response.

Table A.1 Understanding Eye Movements

Eye movement	What clue this gives about how the information is processed	The phrases or words that might cue this
Straight ahead defocused	**Visualization:** usually this person is having an *associated* visual experience—that is, seeing it through their own eyes. This situation could be an actual memory or simply a very intense "fantasy."	"Imagine you are an abused woman standing by the telephone wondering if you dare call the helpline or if your violent partner might see you calling. Your donation shows you want to help that woman."
Up to *their* right	**Visual constructed images:** usually this person is *imagining* an experience visually. So they are having to *create* the experience or image.	"I want you to picture the look on the woman's face when she arrives at the door of the refuge, knowing she'll be safe once she crosses the threshold. Your gift will make sure that door is always open."
Up to *their* left	**Visual remembered images:** usually this person is recalling a *real* visual experience that they have had—that is, they're *re-creating* a picture of an actual situation they've been in or seen.	"I don't know if you've ever had the experience of being in a situation where you could see no way out and you were looking for help from a friendly face?" [Pause to check that they are retrieving such a memory.] "Your investment in the refuge will ensure there's always an open door when a desperate woman needs help."
Sideways to *their* right	**Auditory constructed sounds:** usually this person is *imagining* a sound. ("Sound" can mean anything from a ringing telephone to a conversation.) As with visual-constructed, they are having to create the experience.	"It's hard to describe the calls we sometimes take on the helpline. Often they need more than a friendly ear to listen—they need practical advice on what to do. Imagine having to tell these women we can't help because we don't have the bed-spaces. Your donation will help us to never have to say 'no' to a battered woman again."
Sideways to *their* left	**Auditory remembered sounds:** usually this person is recalling a *real* sound—music, a conversation they have had, and so on. They are *re-creating* an actual experience they've been in where sound was important.	"Can you remember a voice from your childhood that scared you or made you anxious? We have women coming to us every day terrified by the noise of a key being inserted into a lock, who jump if a noisy kitchen chair is pushed back too abruptly. To them, those sounds mean their partner is back and odds are the terrible shouting will start.

Table A.1 (continued)

		With your donation we can speak up for these women."
Down to *their* right 😊	**Kinaesthetic remembered (feelings and bodily sensations):** this person is usually retrieving a *real* feeling experience. This might be an emotion—sadness, joy, embarrassment—or a smell or how something physically feels (cold clammy hands, being too hot).	"Can you remember ever feeling really alone? I guess most of us have at some point in our lives. At times like that it's essential that you know there is somewhere safe you can go, where you'll be welcomed. The refuge provides not only security but emotional support."
Down to *their* left 😊	**Auditory digital (internal dialogue):** this person is usually talking to themselves silently—saying perhaps 'oh no, you messed up again.' Internal dialogues are often negative.	"You may be saying to yourself— 'I'm already too involved in too many causes. I can't get involved in another.' But I want you to think how you'd answer those women if you were taking calls on the refuge helpline."

Also, eye movements can sometimes be very quick or quite subtle in between people making eye contact with you. So someone can briefly remember a feeling by looking down and then "come back" to talk to you almost instantly. You need to pay careful attention to their eyes—without staring, obviously!

When looking for eye cues, also be careful to note the following:

- The same event might produce a number of movements. So the question "What color sweater did you wear yesterday?" might lead the person to think first of how angry they were that someone spilled ink on their sweater *before* they recall the color. In other words, their eyes might move down to their right (kinaesthetic remembered) before moving up to their left (visual remembered).

- Although the cues are *generally true*, it's more impor-tant to focus on the individual you wish to influence and try to work out what *their* pattern is. It might

just be different for them—for example, movements are often reversed in left-handed people. You
should match the real situation, not the theory.

- Be aware that eye contact is itself a powerful communication
element central to building rapport. Note too that rapport is
generally more important than trying to find out the way in
which information is being processed through the eye cues.

We're guessing you might be feeling slightly overwhelmed
by all this information on eye movements. Again, we want to
reassure you that this is something you can pick up easily with
practice. If you're an experienced car driver, try to remember what
it was like when you learned to drive. At first it was tough having
to manage what was going on inside the car as well as being aware
of the traffic and pedestrians outside. Now you *unconsciously* take
in and respond to internal and external events and information,
moving aside to let another car pass without being aware of it,
adjusting your speed according to the surroundings. In time, you'll
become equally unconsciously competent at taking account of
people's eye movements—providing you work at it.

Appendix B

USING RICHER LANGUAGE

Richer or more vivid language will help make your case more powerful. And one way to make your language more powerful is to use metaphors and similes. These are a well-established way to create impact. They're used in everything from novels to the bible, comic books to poetry. At their best they help make your ideas or messages memorable, and create a powerful emotional response in the donor.

Let's be clear what we're talking about. If you studied Shakespeare at school you may remember the famous lines from *As You Like It*:

"All the world's a stage
And all the men and women merely players."

That's a *metaphor*—directly relating life to a stage and people to actors, identifying *similarities*.

A *simile* is a related but slightly different version of the same idea. In a simile you tend to say more indirectly how something is *like* something else. Shakespeare also used these. Take this description of Julius Caesar:

"Why man he doth bestride the narrow world like a Colossus"

Both metaphor and simile are common in our everyday communication, and are used frequently in pop songs: "You are my sunshine" (metaphor) or "Your eyes are like the sun" (simile).

The useful thing about these forms of speech is that they don't need to relate to issues directly in our experience. For example, you may have noticed that a number of nautical metaphors are used in work settings, whether or not people have been to sea. You might hear a colleague say, "The CEO nailed her colors to the mast in that speech!" or "We need to batten down the hatches financially," or "We came through the service assessment shipshape."

So metaphors and similes are useful. However, you also need to understand that a specific metaphor or simile will have a different impact on different people. How an individual responds depends on his or her sensory language preference—visual, auditory, or kinaesthetic—as explored in Chapter Eight. Ideally, what you want is a single metaphor that encapsulates all three preferences, such as the Bolivian priest's brick in Chapter Four. That had

- The physical brick held in the hand of the priest as a *visual* reminder of the negative consequences of illiteracy (visual)
- The *sound* as the brick was slammed on the table and the boy *saying*, "This book is useless" (auditory)
- The *feeling* of the vibration as the brick hit the table and also the *distress* of the priest at the conse-quences of poverty and illiteracy (kinaesthetic)

You'll find your communication becomes more effective gen-erally if you use even simple metaphors in your fundraising language. Often a word or phrase will capture an idea more strongly than will pages of closely written text.

Following are some examples of rich or vivid language, many of which use also metaphors or similes. You can use this list to help you think about some better ways to express your ideas, or you can use it to help spot language preferences in donors.

Note that these are not great literary metaphors as in the Shakespeare examples. Some may sound like clichés. The reality is that people do often talk in cliches—but even these can help us share information.

Kinaesthetic Language

- The committee gave his ideas a *warm* reception.
- Things are going *smoothly* in terms of the campaign after a rocky start.
- They savored the *sweet smell* of success after the gala event.
- He worked at a *feverish* pace to finish the annual plan outline.
- They had a *heated* debate about the ethics of online fundraising.
- Her *bubbly* personality was great at cultivation events.
- The behavior of the consultant was a *painful* lesson in my fundraising career.
- She was *boiling* mad about the way her gift had been acknowledged.
- He was being *pressured* to decide on the grant.
- The idea of the presentation at the foundation conference left her *frozen* with fear.

Visual Language

- She *lit* up the room when she met the fundraising volunteers.
- There's an infinite *spectrum* of possibilities for your sponsorship.
- The initiative was a *brilliant* idea and raised $500,000.
- The team took a *dim* view of the restructure.
- My memory's a bit *cloudy* on what was decided at the development committee.

- The annual fund plan still seems a little *hazy*.
- The stewardship program is a *shining* example of best practice.
- Our development director is a *beacon* for fellow workers.
- The presentation got a *glowing* review.
- He always seemed a *shady* character in the sponsorship world.

Auditory Language

- The world is *listening*.
- Her *words* at the AGM *rang* true.
- The proposal was *music* to his ears.
- The *high note* of the evening was the celebrity auction.
- She *thundered* into the boardroom to give the volunteers a hard time.
- The logo says "We're *in touch* with youth."
- The fundraising case was *gobbledygook* to me.
- We want to *talk turkey* about the sponsorship ideas.
- There's a *whisper* around the office that there's a restructure planned.
- Thanks for the proposal—I need to *talk it over* in my head.

Appendix C

TRANSLATING YOUR CASE—MATCHING PREFERENCES IN PROPOSALS

This appendix features a case study of an imaginary U.S. charity, ChildCare. It is designed to illustrate the impact of matching elements in your fundraising case to different audiences with different thinking preferences. Specifically, it builds on the sensory and metaprograms preferences discussed in Chapters Eight and Ten. The case study is based on some real work we did for a U.K. customer.

The advantage of preparing this kind of material in advance is that you can quickly bring together ideas for a leaflet or e-mail if you're stuck for inspiration—or if the donor's preference is not one you share. The alternative is to rely on your own flexibility in a live situation. We prefer the preparation.

Imagine you're an employee of ChildCare. ChildCare is a child protection charity that also provides support to parents who are concerned that, under stress, they might harm their own children.

The charity's work is designed to

- End child abuse, including sexual abuse and trafficking
- End child neglect where children are not properly cared for
- Create safe opportunities for children to grow and develop
- Enable parents to feel safe disclosing the frustrations they sometimes feel

You need to create a set of mini case statements or fundraising propositions that will meet the psychological preferences of a range of different donors. To do this you decide to systematically translate elements of the work the charity does in two ways. The first is into different sensory systems—visual, auditory, and kinaesthetic (see Chapter Eight, "Speaking the Language of Influence"). The second is into the most common metaprograms (see Chapter Ten, "Helping Donors Say 'Yes'").

Translating an Appeal into Sensory Systems

This first section breaks down the broad appeal elements into kinaesthetic, auditory, and visual sensory systems. It also includes the concept of a *problem* that the donor might care about, and the *solution* to which the donor could contribute.

Kinaesthetic

The Problem of Children Left Alone

"You're five years old. Imagine how it feels to be shut away by yourself in a cold, damp bedroom while your parents go out for a drink with their friends. Help us to rescue this five-year-old, and all the others like her, who are alone and neglected."

The Problem of Parents' Feeling Isolated

"Many parents, especially young parents, feel overwhelmed by the pressures of parenthood—the night-time feeds, the child that won't sleep, the baby that never seems to stop crying. When the pressure gets too much to bear, it often comes out as violence and anger. Violence and anger that's, sadly, directed against the children the parents love—a frustrated shake, a tap that turns into a slap. Help us to help the parents. Help us to keep the children safe."

The Solution of Creating Child-Friendly Zones in Every City

"Like you, I'd like to feel that every child can play and enjoy themselves safely. That's a fundamental right! ChildCare's network of child-friendly zones will provide that secure environment."

The Solution of Giving Every Adult a Booklet to Help Stop Child Abuse

"Last year our volunteers trudged around the streets of the United States in all kinds of weather, hand-delivering 750,000 copies of a booklet on good parenting that's designed to stop violence against children in the home. That's one booklet to every fifth home. But there is still a long way to go. There are still many parents who haven't had access to the sensible, down-to-earth advice that's in the booklet. We need your help to make sure every parent in America has a copy at hand whenever they need it."

 Auditory

The Problem of Parents' Needing Help to Deal with Stress

"We all need someone to talk to. But if you're a mother at the end of your tether, who can you talk to about how guilty you feel about shouting at your child? Who'll listen? Who won't pass it on as gossip?"

The Problem of Helping Children Who Are Living in Abusive Settings

"A child crying is one of the most distressing sounds you can hear. But after talking to our specialist researchers, we reckon almost a thousand abused children's calls for help go unheard every day. You can help us answer those cries for help."

The Solution of Giving Parents Access to Skilled Social Work Help

"Psychologists say that when parents get into a cycle of arguments it's often the children who are most affected by the verbal violence. Parents need professional advice to break the cycle. Talking things through with a skilled ChildCare social worker means at last there's someone to listen. The parents are taught to avoid the shouting matches at home that cause emotional pain. Help us to provide the caring, listening ear."

The Solution of Providing a Telephone Helpline

"Every telephone in the ChildCare helpdesk rings fifty times a day with calls from adults and children pleading for help. By enabling us to talk to those people you're helping answer those cries. I'm asking you for $20 a month to help keep a trained counselor listening for an hour."

Visual

The Problem of the Hidden Scale of Child Abuse

"The photographs tell the tale—young children, their bodies covered in bruises from head to toe, the sparkle gone from their dulled eyes. But we can't simply close our eyes to the truth in those photos. Out of sight mustn't mean out of mind."

The Problem of Child Abuse Being an Everyday but Ignored Phenomenon

"Imagine you glanced out of the window and saw someone hitting a three-year-old with a stick. You wouldn't look away and pretend it wasn't happening, you'd see what you could do to stop it. But the problem is that most child abuse takes place hidden behind closed doors and drawn curtains. And most people don't imagine it's as big a problem as it is—despite the evidence staring us in the face."

The Solution of Putting Out TV Ads to Draw Attention to the Issue

"You know what it's like to open a newspaper and see those dreadful headlines. Or to switch on the TV and witness the anxious faces of parents, blinking back tears and looking out of the screen seeking for some glimmer of hope about their abducted child. The new campaign provides a really clear way forward to keep children out of harm's way."

The Solution of Ensuring That Every Child Involved in a Court Case Has a "Supporting Adult" to Defend Their Interests

"Imagine a child preparing to give evidence in an abuse case. That child could have to describe in graphic detail their experience in front of the very adult responsible for their abuse. ChildCare is looking for the finances to provide every child with an independent, trained social worker to watch over their interests during the ordeal. You could help to provide a professional caregiver to look after that child in court with your gift of $1,200."

Translation into Metaprograms

In this section we have translated a number of the *problems* and *solutions* that ChildCare is seeking support for into three of the key metaprograms—or information-processing preferences—that donors have. These are

- Toward or away from
- Big chunk or small chunk
- Past, present, future

Note that in the original material these were also then clustered into visual, auditory, and kinaesthetic.

Toward and Away From

Some people prefer messages in terms of *avoiding the negative*, and some prefer messages in terms of *working toward the positive*. This has important implications for ChildCare when you draft your case.

Away From	*Toward*
"We've got to end this nation's dreadful history of ignoring child abuse. It's a scandal we have to leave behind us."	"We're working toward a society in which children are at the heart of everything we do—and every child has a future."
"Many parents still have a lot of old-fashioned and negative attitudes toward children, and we've got to get rid of those attitudes. Smacking children is never okay."	"Many loving parents want to step up and grasp the opportunity to find out about supportive ways to bring up children. We need to push forward with sharing ideas."
"We're looking at a situation that many fairy tale writers would recognize: children are treated as something to be seen, not heard."	"We need to build bridges to the future—focus on creating a framework in which children are accorded the same rights as adults."

Big Chunk or Small Chunk

Some people like to think in terms of big chunks. Other people like to think in terms of detail or smaller chunks. You decide to frame up the ChildCare message in these ways.

Big Chunk	*Small Chunk*
"Child abuse is the biggest single threat to young people in our society. Every year almost 100,000 are subjected to abuse. Imagine our local baseball stadium with all the spectator seats filled with abused young people—that's the scale of the problem."	"In a street of twenty houses right here in this neighborhood there's a probability that in one house a child is being hurt. Maybe you can't stop the abuse. But with your help we can rescue that one child. And that's a start. Every single child needs individual help."

Big Chunk	Small Chunk
"We want to change the whole way society thinks about children and their needs and rights. That's a massive cultural undertaking. And that's why we're running training programs across the United States."	"We want to change the attitudes of individual people you know—the postman, the shopkeeper, the bus driver, your aunt. You can help change their point of view. That's how most change starts—one person at a time."

Past, Present, Future

Some people build from the past, some are concerned about the present, and some emphasize the future. So you need to frame your proposal in this way.

Past "How long is it since we agreed as a society that children should be able to grow up safe and secure? Fifty years? We've really made relatively little progress since the Second World War."

"Think back over the past week. What have you bought—a round of drinks, a pastry you didn't eat—and afterwards thought "What a waste of money"? Could that money have helped answer one of the twenty calls the helpline missed this week?"

Present "We have to begin to protect children from being harmed—without delay. Today, as soon as you leave this meeting—I'd like you to write to your congressman and vote for the child protection legislation going through the legislature."

"Put your hand in your pocket or purse. How much do you have in there? How much do you need until you can get to an ATM? We could use that money *now*. ChildCare needs $50 every minute to have a counselor ready to help children twenty-four hours a day."

Future "I'd like to be able to look forward to 2012 and see a situation in which every child at risk is offered a safe home with foster parents or caregivers and has the chance of a brighter prospect."

"All of ChildCare's projections suggest the same prognosis. Abused children tend to become abusers themselves—we have to break that cycle of harm stretching out into the future."

Appendix D

INFLUENCING IN A GROUP

Many people find it quite threatening to talk to a group of even fifteen or twenty people. The idea of speaking to an audience of five thousand people would cause a heart attack. But influence often demands that we do present to groups. To be successful in such situations you have to adapt to the different needs and demands of the audience. And you need some techniques beyond those discussed earlier in the book.

In this appendix we look at

- The different approaches you need to work with a large group rather than a small group or one-to-one—especially in some key areas such as eye contact
- How to take in the additional data you get from a large group and to build and maintain rapport with them
- How to use different communication techniques to ensure that you meet the range of needs they have

What's Different About Influence in a Group?

Most of this book has been about influence in one-to-one or small-group settings. But you may also need to build rapport and influence in a group of five or even five thousand.

Whether you call it a presentation or a pitch, being able to stand up and convince a *number* of disparate people at the same time to support you is a key skill for fundraisers. We can define a "pitch" as a meeting of an individual and a group, in which the individual presents a message in a persuasive manner in order to achieve a desired outcome. Presentations are particularly important in sponsorship settings because that's a format that many businesses are familiar with and use to make charity investment decisions.

The key differences in a group situation versus one-to-one are

- You have to build rapport by using a *range* of communication styles and preferences
- You may need to identify and meet a range of different interests in one setting and in one communication slot
- You need to manage and organize the structure much more than in a one-to-one setting
- When you hand over to the "audience" for questions, you may have positive *and* negative feedback to manage

When you want to influence a group, you use some of the skills we've looked at for one-to-one influence, plus some very different ones. In our experience there are five broad communications elements you need to consider. These are

1. Body language
2. Gestures
3. Eye contact
4. Living language
5. Use of audiovisual

Adopt Confident Body Language

We've already written quite a lot about body language in Chapter Seven, "Building Rapport," but there are differences when presenting to a group. For a start, you have to accept that by standing up and making a presentation you are separating yourself from the group. So although you can have *rapport*, it's not quite the same as when you're matching one-to-one.

Going back to the ideas in Chapter Seven, you need to work hard to avoid *cognitive dissonance*—when you unconsciously undermine the words you use with inappropriate body language or voice. You can create this dissonance regardless of whether you're telling the truth or lying, though people may interpret it as lying—or uncertainty at best.

We were asked to undertake an organizational review for a social service agency in Wisconsin. The staff were nervous. They had heard that change consultants had been hired. Worse still, a rumor was going around that the phrase "organizational review" was management code for "redundancy program." Hearing of this nervousness, the head of the service offered to introduce us to the hundred-plus staff at a meeting. He was keen to reassure them about the purpose and scope of our project. He stood up and began to speak:

> "Today I'm—er—glad—er—that you've all come to this meeting. I—er—know—er—that some of you are worried that—er—there will—um—will be layoffs. Don't worry at all. The consultants—er, mmm—are going to look for things to review and how we can save money. And they're almost certainly—sorry, absolutely certainly—[cough]—er, mmm—not going to recommend layoffs."

As he spoke he paced around the room. He looked down at the floor or up to the ceiling. He shook and wrung his hands. He coughed. He played with his glasses, obsessively taking them on and off. It wasn't good. The staff were becoming more anxious, not less.

In fact, he was being completely honest. And if you read the *text* of his presentation—cutting out the "ums" and "ers"—you'd find he had given a pretty cast-iron reassurance that our project wasn't anything to be worried about. But his inappropriate body language and the verbal rambling seriously undermined the clear and simple message. That's cognitive dissonance.

Cognitive dissonance *can* also occur when someone is lying. Some popular body language books have oversimplified common actions. For example, people often touch their noses or scratch inappropriately when they are nervous. A poorly researched body language book would say, "When people scratch their nose while talking they are lying." As an absolute, *that is not true*. The touching or itching that happens when we're nervous is a *physiological response* to anxiety, and is due to blood flowing to the surface of the skin. Being *nervous* is not necessarily a sign of lying. However, it *is* true that people will feel a subconscious concern about a speaker who touches or scratches their nose while saying something important.

Famously, for example, former president Bill Clinton touched his nose several times in interviews while repeating the mantra, "I did not have sex with that woman." Now at that point we didn't know if Bill was lying or not. But had we been his body language coach we would have given him some very straightforward advice: "Whether you did or did not have sex with the woman, DON'T TOUCH YOUR NOSE!"

Lying is, in general, *a bad thing*. But sometimes in influence situations you want to conceal your true feelings because they're not appropriate or helpful. For example, you might want to conceal that you feel fed up this particular morning because you had an unpleasant argument with a man in a shop on the way to the meeting. A group of donors is fairly unlikely to care about your personal problems. In our view, concealing unhelpful emotions in an influence situation is not unethical.

Positive Posture Part of the secret of avoiding cognitive dissonance is *positive posture*—the way you hold yourself and stand. Your body is the element of you that your audience sees and experiences the most. Whatever its size, it provides the greatest amount of information about you and how you feel about you and them. And whether you like it or not, in a presentation your audience uses data gleaned from your body language to form their initial opinion of you. That's why positive posture is so incredibly important.

Notice we recommend you *should* stand to present to a group. Although we're all in favor of relaxed situations, our experience suggests that standing signals a formality and distance from the group that's appropriate when you're making a presentation. Otherwise you're having a *meeting*. By standing you indicate you want to control the flow of information for a period of time. When you sit down, this can indicate that the balance of power is now with the audience to ask questions or challenge what you've said.

But there is *good* and *bad* standing. Look around any group of people standing up. You'll see that some stand with their weight on one leg, others with their feet crossed. Some clasp their hands together, and some wave them around. We all have a preferred—or default—way of standing or holding ourselves. And for many of us the challenge is that our default may not be appropriate or helpful for the kind of image we want to project. There are a number of gender-based "tics" in posture—especially under conditions of stress. When they're feeling nervous, men will often respond to their anxiety by adopting a "military" pose with legs quite far apart, toes pointing out, and hands clasped behind the back. This may be off-putting for the audience they're working with. Women, in contrast, often adopt a more passive, "pleasing" stance. Typically, this might involve standing with feet quite close together, head tilted on one side, and with hands clasped in front. This can look a little childlike. Both of these postures are inappropriate if you want to be regarded as a strong, sensible adult.

The ideal position is called the neutral or ready position, and if you're making a pitch or presentation we suggest you adopt it. It's important to say this is a position we've tested worldwide, and everywhere it seems to convey an impression of self-confidence without arrogance or apology.

When you first start to use it, this neutral position can feel weird and unnatural. However, it has a good pedigree, being similar to the basic posture used in Tai Chi known as "touching the earth." And, as with the Tai Chi position, it does indeed make you feel *grounded*. This is not a position to stay in through the whole presentation—you can move! But if you adopt it at the beginning of the presentation, it will help to steady your nerves (and make you appear confident). And if you return to it after completing a gesture or movement it will give the gesture or movement more definition—and more impact.

Getting into Neutral

- *Stand, and stand upright:* It's important to stand, for two reasons. One is to separate yourself from the group you're presenting to. After all, you are claiming the right to be heard. The other is that by standing you give the audience access to the 55 percent information that your body offers. (See Chapter Seven, "Building Rapport.")

- *Adopt the neutral or ready position:* Stand with your weight evenly balanced, and your feet parallel, shoulder-width apart. This posture gives you a sense of being grounded. If the feet are closer together you can end up being off balance. Further apart, and you can appear slightly aggressive.

- *Move your* upper body *and keep your lower body still:* We gain the sense of commitment and energy from upper body movement. So feel free to move from your waist up, but below that try to keep still. In this way you give the impression of being dynamic but centered. Try it and see.

Let's reiterate. We're not saying you need to stay completely still. You can—and indeed should—move. Good, purposeful movement is helpful to you and your audience to create a sense of dynamism. But the movement must *be* purposeful *and* appropriate rather than unconscious pacing or jiggling on the spot. As you'd expect, we have some principles for *movement* to complement those for posture:

- *Claim the space*: This is a phrase borrowed from acting. Actors say the hardest thing to do is to walk onto an empty stage and stand in the middle as though you had a perfect right to be there. There's a similar process for you as a presenter. When you move into a space—for example, to present to a board or committee sitting in a U-shaped layout of tables—move confidently to the most open and exposed space available as though you own it.

- *Use GPS (Great Presenting Spots)*: Identify three or four key places in the room. Make these your GPS locations. Give each of these places a role or function. When we're coaching fundraisers to influence in a group, we'll usually suggest they have a "serious" spot, a "funny" spot, and a "visionary" spot. Using GPS means that when you have a particular type of message, you deliver it from that spot. Try it. Rather like Pavlov and his dogs, after a while you can "train" your audience to be ready for something serious or funny or aspirational just by standing in the right place in the room.

- *Practice WST (Walk, Stop, and Talk)*: Avoid talking *while* you walk. By all means, walk to one of your GPS places and then say something. If you talk *while* you walk you run the risk of trying to communicate when you're actually facing away from a key decision maker. This makes it impossible to spot their reaction. The rule is simple. *Walk* in silence to the spot where you want to communicate your next message. *Stop* and reengage with the audience. Then share your message. It might seem like a long time between moves but there are huge benefits to be gained by *not saying anything*. See "Use Living Language and Meaningful Pauses" to find out more.

Finally, don't forget that your pitch may well take place in unfamiliar surroundings. It's much better if you can familiarize yourself with the space you'll present in. Try to find out in advance what the layout and setup will be, because then you'll be able to mentally rehearse for that. Even if you can't do that, it's essential that you establish the placement of potential "obstacles" such as flipchart stands or random pieces of office or boardroom furniture.

Make Gestures for Impact

Body posture offers a strong overall impression of how you feel about yourself and the audience. *Gestures* are a more specific aspect of body language using hand movements to reinforce ideas or feelings. They work best when they're used for emphasis at key points. A strong and well-chosen gesture stays in the mind longer than purple prose.

We all do a certain amount of—often unconscious—gesturing in the normal course of conversation. What we're talking about here is deciding to reinforce one or more key ideas or messages through conscious use of your hands. This kind of *gesture* achieves impact through a three-stage approach:

- *Decide* on a key point that would benefit from gesture reinforcement. Plan it. Rehearse it. Be ready to repeat the gesture when you repeat the point.

- *Magnify* it—make it much bigger than in normal conversation. Push the envelope. If you pay attention to the audience they will tell you when it's too big.

- *Hold it* for emphasis, and to plant it in the audience's mind, keep the gesture going for longer than maybe feels comfortable to you.

There are two different kinds of gestures that we tend to use when communicating—we call them "sells" and "tells."

Selling Gestures As the name suggests, these are gestures that "sell" ideas, or help to make a notion or concept more concrete. So after a run of poor productions, the artistic director of a theater might say to a group of donors, "We have to fight our way back to the top of the league in terms of artistic quality." He could accompany the metaphor by beginning with a very low gesture with his left hand, followed by a more sweeping upward movement with his right hand toward the imaginary "artistic" target at the top of the league. Use *selling* gestures sparingly in your presentation. But use them. Make them specific. And don't be afraid to repeat them when you've moved on in the presentation. Back to our artistic director: "So how can we get back to the top of the league? (*repeat right-hand gesture*) Let me tell you my plan—and how I'd like you to help."

Telling Gestures These are gestures that express how you feel to the audience you're speaking to. The classic open arms that accompany "Welcome" is a *tell*. The spread arms signal your openness and willingness to engage with them. You can also touch yourself (especially with one hand flat against the chest) to express emotion—"I'm sorry to hear about your mother's illness." "I feel passionately that we need to do more to help lone parents." This self-touching is connected to the kinaesthetic system discussed in Chapter Eight. So our artistic director might say, "I have to admit I'm anxious." And touch himself on the chest. And then go on to say, "I need your help. All of you," at the same time using an open hand to indicate the donors in the room.

When you're planning to make a presentation, follow these three rules for gestures:

- Decide what your *key messages* are and consider having a *specific gesture* that matches the idea you're going to sell.
- Practice your gestures in advance. This won't make you fake or inauthentic. It will make you appear more in control and professional.
- Be sparing with the really big gestures. It's not necessary to have a gesture for every idea—you're not audio describing for a hearing-impaired audience, or miming.

Use Eye Contact for Rapport

Eye contact is a very important part of influence. You *should* make eye contact. (Though be aware the rules are slightly different if you're making a pitch or presentation than in a one-to-one setting.) It's one of the main indicators of your level of confidence, but there are many myths about it.

Actually eye contact is a bit of a misnomer. Most people use the phrase when they really mean "gaze"—that is, the way in which we look at others and they look back at us. People use "gaze" in different ways and for different reasons, and like it in different amounts.

It seems a pretty tall order to match the eye contact preferences of every individual in a group, but it *is* possible with up to fifteen people. The secret of success is to focus (pardon the pun) on them. Engage with the group as individuals. And rather than thinking about how nervous *you* feel, put your energy into watching them and noticing how they are responding to your proposition. As you look at each person, you will discover how much eye contact they want by their blinking. When they blink, move on to someone else. (Notice too how you can gain a clue into what people are thinking by their eye movements—see Appendix A.)

In a big group presentation—over fifty people—you can manage rapport and impact by using a different approach to eye contact. Essentially you have to look at a "group" within the audience as you make a specific point. It doesn't matter which group you look at for the point. But look at that space or group. Then move and look at a different group within the audience, make a new point, and move on. For the time you're looking at a particular group, they will feel you are looking at them and that will make them feel important.

One of the easiest ways to do this is to look methodically for the "Lady in Red." Look for someone—woman or man—wearing something red. Focus on them and share your key point. All the audience members sitting around that person will feel you're looking at them. Then search for someone else wearing red, and share your next idea with them. And so on. (Any color or gender will do!) It will *look* natural and as if you are genuinely keen to connect with those you're working to influence.

There are some common eye contact problems people have when they are presenting. Typically these are

- *Concentrating on props.* Props, such as notes, flipcharts, screens, PowerPoint images, and so on, can take your attention away from the audience. Notes are especially distracting for an audience, particularly shaking ones in the hands of a nervous presenter. At first people worry that the presenter might lose the plot, and if it continues, they can get irritated and stop listening.

- *Looking over people's heads.* Because the audience is sitting down and you're standing, it's easy—and can feel more com-fortable for you—to look at the wall, or out of the window behind them. But it is very distracting and unsettling for an audience, who can feel as if you're not very interested in them. *Where* you look when you lose eye contact—up at the ceiling, straight ahead, down at the floor—is an indication of the way you prefer to store and retrieve information (again, see Appendix A, "Accessing Eye Cues.")

- *Looking down at the carpet or your feet.* This is sometimes a sign of a negative internal dialogue with yourself, or too strong an emotional connection to your subject. Be care-ful that you don't get into this habit. It makes you focus internally, and encourages negative inner feelings. Audi-ences tend to find excessive emotion uncomfortable. There's also the danger they may think you've got something to hide because you won't make eye contact with them.

- *Making too little eye contact.* This can leave your audience feeling uncertain if you're interested in or really talking to them. Remember that "enough" is as much as they want. This can mean very different things to different cultures, genders, and sexualities. Make sure you offer enough contact to signal interest in them and to access their reaction to you.

- *Creating prisoners.* This refers to the habit of focusing your attention on one or two people. There are two types of "prisoners." One is when an individual gives you so much positive feedback—smiling, nodding encouragement—that the rest of the group seems negative. It's only natural to concentrate on the person who appears to like you. The second is when someone looks away, sits glowering at you, or appears more interested in doodling than in what you're saying. As presenters we take responsibility for this, when in fact the person is simply distracted by something that happened to them earlier. Avoid both forms of prisoner focus—you could lose the rest of your audience.

If you make good eye contact through appropriate gaze you'll also gain other advantages that are useful in your influence goal. Our research shows that people will perceive you as honest, sincere, confident, and empathetic.

Use Living Language and Meaningful Pauses

This key skill is concerned with the *content* of your pitch or presentation—the words you use and the spaces in between. There are universal challenges that can affect verbal delivery: speaking too quickly; using jargon or inappropriate language; using nonwords or fillers such as "um," "er," "y'know"; gabbling or stuttering; using the wrong word.

Many of these are the result of a physiological *fight or flight* response. If you're badly affected by nerves when you pitch, and that affects how well you remember—and deliver—your words, try using the anchoring techniques we talked about in Chapter Six, "Building Self-Confidence." But remember, if the people you're pitching to weren't basically interested in what you have to say, you wouldn't have been given the opportunity to present in the first place. Most of us can speak completely coherently provided we're clear about what we want to say. Above all avoid writing it all out in longhand—written language is very different from spoken, and you will sound scripted and false.

Successful presentation language depends on the "3S Principles." Keep your language

- *Simple*: Don't use high falutin' words that will get in the way of your message! Use ones that are familiar and easy to understand. Review Chapter Four, on writing.
- *Suitable*: Use vocabulary that is appropriate to the audience. Look for opportunities to bring in their favorite words—do they talk about a "donation" or a "social investment"?
- *Sensory*: Use words to create a rich tapestry of your project or proposition. Make it come alive for the listener. Talk in colors. Evoke smells and tastes. Capture sounds. Essentially these are the visual, auditory, and kinaesthetic modalities we discussed in Chapter Eight.

There is a fourth element to successful spoken communication that parallels the nonverbal *neutral* position. When you're not sure what to say, or when you're worried you might find yourself using awkward nonwords such as "um," or "hmm," or "you know," there is an alternative to filling the space unproductively. And that's to leave the space empty. This wonderfully powerful tool is called *pausing*.

Use Power Pauses Pausing harnesses the power of silence. Apart from banishing your nonwords, a power pause

- Creates time for *you*—to collect your thoughts and decide what to say next rather than gabble on hoping the words will come.

- Makes time for *them*—allowing your audience to absorb and store important information you've just given them—they can decide how they *feel* about your ideas.

- Aids transitions between *different subject matters*—for example, "So that covers the *social* implications." PAUSE. "But what about the *educational* implications?"

- Helps transitions between *different tones*—moving from serious issues to lighter ones can be made easier by combining the pause with an appropriate movement to a new GPS.

- Emphasizes the importance of something by acting as a kind of verbal gesture—use pauses on either side of key messages to draw attention to them.

- Creates drama—for example, "What could your $500,000 do to help AIDS orphans in West Africa?" PAUSE. "Let me tell you ..." The drama pulls people in and makes the answer more compelling.

The "punctuation" of your language, using pauses, controls the *pace* of your presentation. Make sure you pay attention to this formula: *Language + Pauses = Pace*. Influence will be helped by pausing.

Have Audiovisual Backup

There are a range of professional audiovisual aids (AVs) available to help *reinforce* the content of your pitch. Using AVs is an accepted technique in business influence situations—so potential commercial sponsors are likely to expect it.

Other general benefits of good AVs include

- Everyone receiving the same message at the same time
- Brevity—a picture speaks a thousand words
- Reinforcement—a memory aid for the key ideas

- Variety of information and format
- Both you and the audience receiving a breather from your talking

The most common audiovisual aid is PowerPoint. Used well, it is effective. But it can be a problem. PowerPoint is being *overused* in many situations, especially the custom animation—snazzy, zippy, special effects. The question is, How many times does your audience want to see text fade in on the screen, spin around, and change color? How does that add value to the ideas on the slide? How does it affect influence? Remember that your audiovisual should be a backup, not a substitute.

For a good example of how to use multimedia PowerPoint, watch Al Gore's film, *An Inconvenient Truth*. The graphics and carefully chosen images perfectly complement the presentation. Remember, he used to be perceived as a wooden presenter.

You can also think about using scale models, audiotapes, and samples as audiovisual support. We refer to a couple of nice examples in Chapter Four that you might like to look at—one using crumbling film stock to illustrate the urgency of the appeal for a conservation project. Likewise, we've seen Greenpeace bring a harpoon into a room and ask donors to imagine the pain that this vicious device inflicts on whales. If you can allow people to touch objects, it creates strong emotional engagement.

Make It Personal

Consider the difference in impact between two approaches to sharing information using audiovisuals. We were doing a fundraising project with a big animal charity in Guatemala that rescued stray animals in the capital, Guatemala City.

The staff of the charity wanted to show some shocking pictures of cruelty as part of a pitch to a small group of concerned donors. Their idea was to project individual images onto a big screen to persuade the donors to fund a shelter where such animals could be looked after. That's a good idea, we said, but we asked them to consider an alternative.

We asked if they had one case that was shocking, recent, and for which they had a series of photographs. Yes, they said, there had been a case in the past few months in which twenty dogs had been found terribly maltreated in a house in a suburb. Ten of the dogs had to be put down because they were too ill to survive. As part of the evidence for a subsequent prosecution, the charity had documented shocking scenes inside the house showing starving, filthy, injured dogs and piles of excrement.

We asked them to create for each donor a copy of a case file like the one they had in their office filing cabinet. We asked them to include facsimiles of the reports from the different professionals involved—the vet, police, staff, and so on. So it looked exactly like the "real" file. Each file also contained a brown envelope with a "disturbing material" sticker on the outside. And inside the envelope was a set of horrific pictures, actually printed on "proper" glossy photographic paper, showing the dogs and the conditions they were found in. As a final touch, the photos had what looked like handwritten notes on the back giving the names of the animals, their ages, and conditions.

The file served as the audiovisual structure for the presentation. The CEO talked people through the file using the pictures to highlight the case. The vet then used a different section of the file with copies of treatment notes for her contribution. And at the back was a reproduction of the various bills and receipts, used by the director of development to illustrate the cost of helping these animals.

So each potential donor had their own file of "evidence" and their own sets of photographs to take home. It felt to them as though they had been in on the investigation.

Remember that *you* are the most powerful audiovisual aid available. You personally can combine words, sound, and images in a responsive and targeted way.

Summary

You may not relish the idea, but presentations are an essential part of your influence approach.

There might be only one person in the room of five hundred people that you need to actively engage—the CEO of the foundation, or the major donor sitting at the back, or the potential corporate sponsor. Or there might be five hundred—all the members of your Friends Committee concerned about the constitutional change, or the half-marathon runners not sure if they should go ahead with the race now that it's raining, or the reluctant bidders in the charity gala auction.

In any event, whether it's one person in the audience or the whole audience, you need to be able to control your nerves and to communicate effectively through five key elements. These are

1. Body language
2. Gestures
3. Eye contact

4. Living language
5. Use of audiovisual

Notes

1. Many of the people we coach complain that keeping their lower body still for a long period of time feels "unnatural." There's a good physiological reason for this. The human body is keyed up to kick into the primitive but powerful *fight or flight* response whenever it feels threatened or nervous. And whether your reaction is to run (flight) or to prepare to defend yourself (fight), your body reckons you need energy. So your brain sends a chemical messenger to your liver to tell it to produce a lot of a particular type of sugar—glycogen—for your muscles. As a consequence, your body is full of energy that needs to be dissipated. Part of the result of that is that in a presentation we tend to walk around unpurposefully. Working to stay still will help counter this. If you continue to pace, it will come across as anxiety—which isn't very helpful if your aim is to appear calm and confident.

2. It's also important to be aware that the amount and form of eye contact a person wants can be affected by culture, sexuality, and gender. Eye contact varies enormously across cultures and countries. For example, North Americans, who tend to blink slowly, can sometimes seem a little aggressive in a Southeast Asian culture such as Thailand, where people tend to blink very quickly as a mark of respect. (Note that these differences can be measured in tenths of seconds.) Anyone who's been to India knows that it's very common for people on a train to really scrutinize you for a seemingly endless period of time. The temptation is to look away, as it feels quite intrusive. Actually it's just normal, but different.

The great news is that if you go to a foreign country they may not have the same rules as you but they will have rules. You can very quickly pick up what's acceptable in eye contact by watching how other people interact. It's a bit like using a computer in a different country. Sometimes the keys are in a slightly different place because of the way their language is structured.

GLOSSARY

This list is designed to be a guide, for people who are not especially familiar with fundraising or psychology, to some of the more technical terms used in the book.

Acknowledgment   A form of thanks—a letter, a card, or an award—for a *gift* given by a *donor*

Anchor   Applying a stimulus (touch, picture, smell, or sound) so that the resourceful state can be created quickly

Appeal   A specific fundraising program for a defined purpose, such as a new hospital appeal

Ask or Fundraising Ask   See *solicitation*

Associated   Experiencing a past or future experience from your own point of view: seeing, hearing, and feeling as if you are present in that moment; see also *disassociation* and *perceptual positions*

Auditory   One of the key *sensory modalities*, referring to a preference for sounds when processing information; see also *visual* and *kinaesthetic*

Body language   A collection of behaviors that form an important 55 percent of any communication, including stance, gesture, movement, and so on; see also *congruence*

Capital campaign   A fundraising campaign for a specific sum of money to be raised in a given period of time for a specific project—often a building

Case statement or case for support   The detailed written rationale for a fundraising proposition or *campaign*, designed for internal and external *stakeholders*

Chunking	Grouping information by class—bigger or smaller—in order to establish some level of agreement or understanding (for example, from "airplane" chunking up to travel or down to Boeing 747); this is one of a series of *submodalities*
Close	The process at the end of a fundraising ask when detailed agreement is reached with a *donor* over a *gift*
Congruence	The match of a person's *body language* with their voice and words while they are communicating
CSR (Corporate Social Responsibility)	A program of social investment by a commercial company; see also *sponsorship*
Cultivation	A range of activities undertaken with a *prospect* designed to engage them in the organization's work—usually leading to a gift
Deletion	One of a series of internal processes—see also *generalization* and *distortion*—that changes a person's experience of the world; specifically involves removing bits of information from an experience or piece of information
Development	A term most common in the United States to define the process of fundraising; see also *resource mobilization*
Development board	A group of leading volunteers, who are themselves donors, who take responsibility for raising funds to support an organization
Development director	The employed person who leads an organization's *development* or fundraising program
Disassociation	The process of stepping outside the point of view of experiencing the world from your own physical position; see also *perceptual positions*
Distortion	One of a series of internal processes—see also *generalization* and *deletion*—that changes a person's experience of the world; specifically involves drawing an untrue conclusion from an experience or piece of information
Donor	The individual who makes a *gift* to an organization

Donor-centric	The process of putting donors and their needs and interests at the center of an organization's work—shaping your activities around them; see also *stewardship*
Emotional intelligence	A model developed by Daniel Goleman, linked to work by Howard Gardiner, consisting of five components: knowledge of needs, self-awareness, ability to control emotions, empathy, and social skills; see also *multiple intelligences*
Eye cues or clues	The movement of an individual's eyes in specific directions, which indicates the accessing of different ways of thinking, or *sensory systems*
Generalization	One of a series of internal processes—see also *deletion* and *distortion*—that changes a person's experience of the world; involves drawing a broad conclusion from a piece of information or experience
Gift	A sum of money or other asset that the *donor* transfers to an organization—normally assumed to be without expecting significant benefits in return; this lack of benefits normally distinguishes a gift from a sponsorship, grant, or contract
High-net-worth individual	A wealthy person, whose known assets are considerably greater than her or his known liabilities (also known as a *high-value donor*)
High-value donor	See *high-net-worth individual*
Kinaesthetic	One of the key *sensory modalities* referring to a preference for pictures and images when processing information; generally relating to feeling, touching, and smell sensations; see also *auditory* and *visual*
Leadership gift	A large gift—often made early in a campaign or appeal—to raise the sights of other potential major *donors*; links to the concept that a very large proportion of the money raised is likely to come from a small percentage of donors
Leading	Using verbal and nonverbal communication to produce a desired response from another person; usually preceded by *matching* or *pacing* to establish *rapport*

Matching	The process of identifying the key behavior in another individual that will allow you to build *rapport*—a sense of trust and connection with them
Moves management	The *cultivation* of a *prospect* seen as a set of preplanned and managed moves or stages; an old-fashioned behaviorist and mechanistic approach to *cultivation* of donors
Multiple intelligences	A model developed by Howard Gardiner in which individuals have a preference for one or more intelligences rather than the simple measure of IQ; commonly listed as visual, linguistic, musical, physical, logical-mathematical, interpersonal, and intrapersonal (These last two are combined in what is often referred to as Howard Gardiner's model of *emotional intelligence*.)
NLP (Neuro-Linguistic Programming)	A body of thinking developed by Bandler and Grinder which demonstrates that the way in which we think and act can be codified and clarified in terms of the language we use
Outcome	A representation of what we want in a specific context concretely defined in terms of all the sensory systems; to be a *well-formed outcome*, it has also to be stated in positive terms, have defined resources that you can access, be within their control, have sensory evidence, and be worth the effort
Pacing	The act of matching breathing, posture, movement, voice tones, and tempo with someone over time, in order to develop rapport; see also *matching*
Peer	A person of equal status, standing, or wealth to another; seen in the expression "peer-group pressure"
Perceptual positions	The point of view taken by an individual at a given time (The most common perceptual positions are first position: that of the person in their own body; second position: that of the other person in a situation; and third position: that of the person observing themselves and the other from a neutral point. There is a fourth position that involves thinking of the wider context for any interaction. Position 1 is described as *associated* and other positions are described as *disassociated*.)

Philanthropy	A combination of two Greek words meaning "love" and "human being," philanthropy is the act of voluntarily, and without seeking personal benefit, doing good for others
Pledge	A promise that a *gift* will be made at a specific point in the future; often written
Proposition	The key idea that sits at the heart of a case statement; also used instead of the term *case statement*
Prospect	A potential *donor* who is believed to be capable of making a gift at an appropriate level—and who has shown some desire to make one
Prospect research	Research to find out a *prospect's* capacity and willingness to support a cause or organization
Rapport	The process of engaging and holding the trust and interest of another person; can be established either consciously, in which case one person matches key aspects of another's behavior or attitudes, or unconsciously; normally achieved by *matching* or *pacing*
Relationship fundraising	A continuing process of long-term trust building with a *donor* which leads to higher donation levels; concept developed by Ken Burnett in his book *Relationship Fundraising*
Resource mobilization	A term—more common in the developing world—for *fundraising* and other related activities to ensure that a project or organization survives; see also *development*
Resourceful state	A psychological and physiological *state* that implies someone has enough information, flexibility in behavior, and self-confidence to undertake a challenging task or handle a difficult situation
Sensory acuity	The ability to notice and understand the likely meaning of small changes in another person's behavior; very useful in influencing to understand the impact of something you have said or done, and to adjust your behavior in one of the *sensory modalities*
Sensory modalities	The general term to describe the three main ways in which *NLP* suggests individuals process information: *visual*, *auditory*, and *kinaesthetic*

Solicitation	The process of actually asking a *prospect* to support the cause with a *gift*
Sponsorship	The exchange of money for benefits between a commercial company and a charity or nonprofit organization; see also *CSR*
Stakeholder	The general term for someone who has a specific interest or concern in an organization or its work; can include *donors*, staff, board members, and beneficiaries
State	The overall emotional physiological and psychological condition of an individual; most often referred to in the context of a *resourceful state*, meaning you are ready and able to take part in an activity or accept a challenge
Stewardship	The process of treating or communicating with and engaging *donors* after they have made their gift; should go beyond simple thank-you letters, progress reports, and acknowledgments and become a *donor-centric* process
Submodalities	The specific finer distinctions within each of the *sensory modalities* (For example the *visual* sensory modality is made up of brightness, color, and hue; the *auditory* modality is made up of volume, tempo, and timbre; *kinaesthetic* involves touch, texture, intensity, heat, and cold.)
Suspect	A person or organization your *prospect research* shows is capable of making a *gift*, but for whom willingness to give has not been established
Visual	One of the key *sensory modalities* referring to a preference for pictures and images when processing information; see also *auditory* and *kinaesthetic*

BIBLIOGRAPHY

Body Language

Body Communication, Michael Argyle, London: Methuen and Co., 1992.

> A comprehensive introduction to an overview of the field of nonverbal communication and how it relates to other forms of communication. Argyle's book has an academic outlook, but is very good on analyzing behavior issues and not jumping to "easy" conclusions.

Peoplewatching, Desmond Morris, New York: Vintage, 2002.

> Morris is the definitive watcher of people, their behavior and habits, and their personalities and quirks. This book explores how people, consciously and unconsciously, signal their attitudes, desires, and innermost feelings with their bodies and actions. Great for improving your cross-cultural awareness.

Negotiation Skills

Getting to Yes: Negotiating Agreement Without Giving In, Roger Fisher and William Ury, New York: Penguin, 1991.

> A short, practical, easy-to-read guide to the practice of what Fisher and Ury call "principled" negotiation. This was developed from the Harvard Negotiation Project, which studied how political negotiation could go wrong.

Getting Past No, William Ury, New York: Bantam, 1993.

> This book builds on *Getting to Yes* and offers helpful advice on handling the negative side of negotiation—staying in control under pressure, refusing anger and hostility, finding out what the other side really wants, and countering dirty tricks.

Everything Is Negotiable (revised), Gavin Kennedy, New York: Random House Business Books, 2008.

> Kennedy's book is very business- and consumer-oriented in the examples used, but it gives useful advice. There are self-assessment tests at the start of each chapter with author answers given at the end of the chapter, with a suggested score. Other features include a helpmail service for readers, five negotiating scenarios, and a two-hour MBA-level negotiating exam.

Harvard Business Essentials Guide to Negotiation, Adviser: Michael Watkins, Boston: Harvard Business School Press, July 2003.

> A thorough book that covers preparing the necessary information before a negotiation, assessing positions, determining your sources of power and authority in a negotiation, and recognizing the barriers to agreement and how to overcome them.

Neuro-Linguistic Programming

Introducing Neuro-Linguistic Programming: Psychological Skills for Understanding and Influencing People, Joseph O'Connor and John Seymour, London: Thorsons, 1993.

> A useful, comprehensive *introduction* to the theory and practice of NLP and how it applies to influence and developing personal confidence and competence. The book does not cover some of the later developments in NLP thinking and theory.

Influencing with Integrity: Management Skills for Communication and Negotiation, Genie Laborde, New York: Syntony, 1988.

> A well-written book with a business-situation bias reflecting the author's experience in commercial communication. It has a useful model—NLP-based—which helps you establish clear out-turns for yourself and others. It also has a number of simple but effective exercises that help you develop your influence skills.

NLP at Work, Sue Knight, London: Nicholas Brearley, 1995.

> A clear and readable guide that explains the terminology and provides advice on how NLP techniques can be put into practical use.

Selling with NLP, Kevin L. Johnson, London: Nicholas Brearley, 1999.

> This is a useful, practical book that takes key elements of NLP and shows their use in commercial sales environments. The link to influence and fundraising in nonprofits is relatively easy to make.

Assertiveness

Assertiveness at Work, Ken and Kate Back, New York: McGraw-Hill, 1991.

> A "classic" that focuses on how to ensure you are able to express your own point of view clearly and unaggressively. Very useful on practical ways to identify and defend what you want in a situation and how to deal with difficult people—colleagues or customers. There are exercises to improve your confidence.

Fundraising-Specific Books

Relationship Fundraising, Ken Burnett, San Francisco: Jossey-Bass, 2002.

> An outstanding work revising and updating the original classic version, this book is essential reading for any fundraiser. It explores the idea that fundraising needs to move beyond transactions to genuine relationships. You'll see evidence of Burnett's work everywhere there's good fundraising.

Asking Properly, George Smith, London: White Lion Press, 1994.

> The definitive work on how language, and especially well-written copy, can transform your case into a powerful ask. Written by one of the leading figures in European fundraising and distilling his knowledge and experience into a readable volume. This also is essential reading for the serious fundraiser.

Training and Coaching

Our company, The Management Centre (=mc), runs training programs in influence for fundraisers and for other nonprofit leaders internationally. We also offer conference presentations in aspects of influence, emotional intelligence, and fundraising.

To find out more, contact us at www.managementcentre.co.uk or b.ross@managementcentre.co.uk or c.segal@managementcentre.co.uk.

THE AUTHORS

Bernard Ross is a codirector of The Management Centre (=mc). =mc is an internationally based management consultancy working exclusively with charities and other nonprofit organizations (www.managementcentre.co.uk).

A prize-winning graduate of Edinburgh University, Ross began his career in community work combating poverty in some of Scotland's toughest housing estates.

He is now a leading authority on fundraising and management in the nonprofit sector. He is involved in consulting and training around the globe in countries as diverse as Australia and Argentina, Sweden and South Africa. He specializes in innovation and strategy but has an abiding interest in the psychology of influence.

He has coached individuals to ask for sums up to $100 million and helped design the presentation that ensured the first woman CEO of Caritas International in its four-hundred-year history.

Clare Segal is also a codirector of =mc. She was a cofounder of =mc almost twenty years ago and has played a leading role in building it up to be a leading player in the consultancy and training world. Clare studied history at York University in the United Kingdom. Before setting up =mc she was an award-winning video producer and director.

Her areas of expertise are communications, interpersonal skills, and personal coaching with charity and NGO leaders.

Among her recent high-profile projects are helping plan for and design the public response to the London bombings in July 2005, helping Save the Children Alliance to raise $500 million for the education of children who live in conflict zones, and facilitating a major review of the U.S. Public Broadcasting System to develop new business models.

She coauthored *Breakthrough Thinking for Nonprofit Organizations* (Jossey-Bass 2002) with Bernard Ross. *Breakthrough Thinking* won the Terry McAdam Award for *Best Nonprofit Book in the USA 2003*—the first time Europeans have won this award.

Index